Living in KINGDOM COME

Living in KINGDOM COME

Vance Havner

Kingsley Press
Shoals, Indiana

Living in Kingdom Come

Published by Kingsley Press
PO Box 973
Shoals, IN 47581
USA

Tel. (800) 971-7985
www.kingsleypress.com
E-mail: sales@kingsleypress.com

ISBN: 978-1-937428-67-9

Copyright © 1967 by Vance Havner

First Kingsley Press edition 2017

This first Kingsley Press edition is published under license from Baker Publishing Group.

All rights reserved. No part of this book may be reproduced or transmitted in any form or by any means, electronic or mechanical, including photocopying, recording or by any information storage and retrieval system without written permission from Baker Publishing Group, except for the inclusion of brief quotations in a review.

Contents

Preface 7
1. Journey from Jugtown 9
2. Living in Kingdom Come 15
3. Notes of a Bugler 23
4. Revival at Shechem 31
5. The Only Christian Nation 37
6. Freedom Through Faith That Follows 41
7. "I Have Set My Face" 45
8. The Christian and This World 49
9. Earthquakes 53
10. Like Him in This World 59
11. Marked Men 67
12. Salt of the Earth 75
13. Knowing What To Do 81
14. Let the Church Be the Church! 87
15. The Bitter-Sweet Book 91
16. The Church Within the Church 97
17. "A Wind From Elsewhere" 103
18. "The Journey Is too Great" 109
19. Despising Our Youth 115
20. Cleansing the Temple 119
21. Bringing Back the King 127

Preface

OF the writing of Havner books there seems to be no end and the reading of them may have become a weariness of the flesh. We feel, however, that so long as messages come to mind and heart and doors open for the preaching of them, we should send them forth in print as well. There may be some repetitions here and there. It is hoped that such "repeats" may be worth saying twice and that there is not too much that was not worth saying once!

In these weird days when the preacher is being manipulated cleverly out of the pulpit and the prophet is being demoted to a mere adviser of sorts, some of us have not resigned our commission but intend to fulfill our ministry which we began when preaching knew better days. We remember one of old who was told by God that while his listeners would hear but not heed, they would know at least and at last that a prophet had been among them. We aspire to that final verdict from our readers but far more to hear our Lord say at the last great day, "Well done … thou hast been faithful."

Vance Havner

Journey from Jugtown

WHEN Abraham's servant started out to look for a wife for Isaac, he prayed for divine guidance. He needed it. A man looking for a wife for himself needs all the light he can get. This man was looking for a wife for somebody else! Later on he said, "I being in the way, the Lord led me..." (Genesis 24:27).

This is my testimony from the summit of the years. I would change that little chorus a bit and sing, "My Lord led the way through the wilderness; all I had to do was to follow."

I grew up in the North Carolina hills. From our front porch we could see at night the lights of five little towns. From the back porch one could see Grandfather Mountain, Table Rock, and companion peaks standing like sentinels along the western skyline. My home community was called Jugtown because in the early years there were little shops up and down the road where potters wrought vessels of clay. I lived the simple, happy life of an old-fashioned country boy. I tramped the woods with a shepherd dog. There was plenty of outdoors, and all the plain joys of rustic youth uncushioned by modern conveniences. It would drive a teenager frantic these days but I thrived on it.

Father was an austere but devout Christian, the pastor's right-hand man at old Corinth Baptist Church. The country preachers always stayed at our house on Saturday before the fourth Sunday in each month, when they came by horse and buggy to preach the monthly sermon. Some of those sermons were long enough to last a month and sounded more like filibusters—but it was sound preaching. Father always let me sit up late on those Saturday nights, before the open fire, and listen to him and the minister talk about the things of God. It beat all the television that has been seen since.

Father should have been a preacher. Two of his brothers did preach – one as a Baptist, the other as a Methodist. Mother was a gentle, kindly soul content to be a housewife. Her life as a "keeper at home" would be anathema to the emancipated woman of today.

I grew up with a Bible in one hand and a bird book in the other. *Pilgrim's Progress, Foxe's Book of Martyrs,* and a set of good classical literature formed our library. I never knew the day when I did not feel that I should preach and write. I memorized Bible portions, made little Sunday school talks, and sent my first "sermon" to our small-town newspaper when I was nine.

When I was ten, I professed faith in Christ. A revival was in progress at Corinth Church, but I came to Jesus alone in the woods. Always following an unbeaten path, I did not go to the mourner's bench as the custom was, but made my decision in a solitary place. There was no dramatic experience such as some can relate; I came as a child in simple trust. I did not understand all about the plan of salvation. I do not understand all about electricity, but I don't intend to sit in the dark until I do.

I was baptized in the South Fork River and a year later I asked the church to license me to preach. I began with a talk at the First Baptist Church of Hickory, twelve miles from my home. I have been in bigger towns and churches since, but none looked as large as did Hickory that night. Dad and I went over in an early Ford with thirty horsepower – twenty of them dead. I stood on a chair and spoke while the pastor of the church stood on one side and the state evangelist stood on the other, like Aaron and Hur holding up the hands of Moses.

For several years I preached on Sundays in town and country churches as a boy preacher. Of course, crowds came out of curiosity. Then I went to a Baptist boarding school called South Fork Institute. I was not a star student, but often sat listening to a bird singing outside rather than to a professor teaching on the inside. I went next to what is now Gardner-Webb College. It was during the First World War. We were singing *Tipperary* and *Over There,* and girl students wept as boyfriends left for camp and for France to make the world safe for democracy. It hasn't been safe for anything since.

The principal of this school advised me, one day, to blaze my own trail instead of following the prescribed course of ministerial training. He told me that I was no genius, but would do well to follow an unbeaten path. I went on to Catawba College for a year, then to Wake Forest. I was restless and wanted to preach. One day, I packed my belongings and left. A professor saw me at the railroad station and said, "Young man, you'll regret this." I haven't regretted it yet. I am not advising others to follow that course, but I believe it was best for me.

I started preaching again, but without guidelines or precedent for my kind of ministry. I made many mistakes, went up blind alleys and dead-end streets. I took a rural pastorate in Eastern North Carolina. I became somewhat enamored of the liberal approach which was beginning to gain favor. It did not become malignant in my case, but I did have enough of the virus in my system to preach popular sermons that convicted nobody. The unbelievers liked my preaching and I had a good crowd, but many of them died unsaved under my ministry.

I resigned after one year and returned to my old home in the hills. Father died that winter, leaving mother and me with a grocery store which was robbed and burned one night. The Lord made it clear to my heart that if I would preach the old message I had proclaimed as a boy, he would make a way for me. I remember reading J. Gresham Machen's *Christianity and Liberalism* out in the woods to my great profit. I returned to the old message, and the first thing I had to do was go back to my country pastorate and preach it for three years. I studied my Bible, tramped the country roads, and laid a good foundation for the years to come. No preacher has had complete preparation who has not been pastor of a country church. It still affords, even in this insane age, some opportunity for meditation and reflection in solitude, that lost art of the modern ministry.

From 1934 to 1939, I was pastor of the oldest Baptist church in the South, the First Church of Charleston, South Carolina. I shall always treasure those five years in that quaint, historic old city. Many blessed experiences were mine, especially a stirring of my heart as to the filling of the Holy Spirit. I was brought to a new dimension by reading *Deeper Experiences of Famous Christians.*

In my country pastorate, I had written my first book, *By the Still Waters.* I wrote for the *Charlotte Observer* and for religious publications. One of them, *Revelation,* edited by Donald Grey Barnhouse of Philadelphia, was helpful in opening doors up north for Bible conferences. Moody Bible Institute's Founder's Week, Winona Lake, Montrose, Maranatha, Pinebrook, Canadian Keswick, and on the west coast, the Torrey Conference in Los Angeles, Mount Hermon and the Firs—these, and many more, eventually appeared on my itinerary. "I being in the way, the Lord led me." No man with God's message need politick, nor pull wires, nor sit hunched over cafeteria tables making contacts, nor wait for some talent scout to find him. He need not chase key men around, if he knows the Keeper of the keys!

So many calls came that I left Charleston and took to the road in 1940. I was in a low state physically, for I had been suffering from nervous exhaustion for two years, and a traveling ministry seemed the last thing a preacher in my condition should undertake. It meant getting adjusted and yet never getting adjusted week after week to different beds, food, climates, environment, and continually rising to the occasion. Yet the way had opened, and I could only go forward.

My first engagement was with the Mel Trotter Mission Bible Conference in Grand Rapids. I got as far as Chicago, came down with the flu, and wound up in a hospital. The devil sat on the foot of the bed and laughed at my discomfiture. The doctor told me to go south. I wired the Florida Bible Institute and accepted an invitation I had declined earlier. There I recuperated, and met the gracious little lady who became my wife and has meant more to me than anyone else on earth. The Lord knew I needed to go south instead of north! Also, in that school I met a lean, lanky student by the name of Billy Graham. We had our pictures taken on the campus. Twenty years later, we posed for another snapshot. What God wrought in twenty years!

I married Sara Allred in 1940, and we took to the road. I could write a book on how the Lord has made a way for us without any conniving on my part. I have seen doors open that I couldn't have pried loose with a crowbar. I have no organization and have never prepared even a brochure for publicity, yet I could have kept another man busy with calls I could not accept. Satan tried to tell me that nobody would stand for my kind of preaching, and that I would starve to death. I look like I'm starving, but I eat three meals a day. I am often reminded of Will Rogers. During the depression of the thirties, when college graduates were walking the streets looking for work, Will was making a good living in his homely way. One day he said to a friend, "It's dinner time and I ain't et." His friend suggested, "You mean you haven't eaten." Will replied, "I notice that a lot of people who haven't eaten *ain't et!*"

From Bible conferences all over the country, and from church revivals, I gradually became occupied almost full time with my own denomination, the Southern Baptists. I had been a Southern Baptist since I was a boy, except for a brief time when I was a member of First Baptist, Minneapolis, Minnesota, while Dr. W. B. Riley was pastor. Dr. Riley baptized my wife, who had been of the Quaker persuasion. I was on a program with Dr. W. A. Criswell of First Baptist, Dallas, in a conference held in the old Baptist Tabernacle of Atlanta, Georgia. Later, I was invited to the Texas Evangelistic Conference for 1949, meeting in First Baptist Church of Dallas. Thus began a new field of ministry in evangelistic conferences, as well as church revivals, all over the convention.

A serious illness in 1960 almost took my life. After major surgery, a blood clot brought me to the door of death. A fine Christian nurse sat by my bed all that night, at her own request, praying and watching. Prayers went up all over the country from Moody Bible Institute to the Florida Baptist Evangelistic Conference where I was to have been speaking. Billy Graham called my wife that night from Miami to say, "We had prayer for Vance and I told my wife that I believed the Lord would let Vance live awhile longer to prepare sermons for the rest of us to preach!" The Lord definitely healed me, and after five months out of the pulpit, I started again in First Baptist of Houston, Texas.

Today, after twenty-seven years on the road, fifty-two years in the ministry, and twenty books, I can only marvel at the way God has gone before me in this journey from Jugtown. Abraham's servant, when he found the wife for Isaac, was invited to linger ten days, but he said, "Hinder me not, seeing the Lord hath prospered my way..." (Genesis 24:56). I am resolved to make that reply when any subtle suggestion arises to take it easy and relax on my heavenly errand. When God has prospered a man's way, he had better be on his way!

> All the way my Savior leads me.
> What have I to ask beside?
> Can I doubt his tender mercy
> Who through life has been my guide?

Retirement age is supposed to mean that I should sit in a rocking chair, wait for my social security check, and reminisce about the good old days. I have no thought of retiring. I would say with Caleb, "give me this mountain"! (Joshua 14:12). I am not asking for molehills. Old soldiers need not fade away. I have asked like Hezekiah for *an extension of time;* like Jabez, for *an enlargement of coast;* like Elisha, for *an enduement of power.* Caleb did not suffer, like the ten frightened spies, from a grasshopper complex. Too many cowards are cringing before the giants of Anak. God give us Calebs looking for mountains to conquer!

Living in Kingdom Come

And have tasted ... the powers of the world to come (Hebrews 6:5).

YEARS ago, there appeared in a popular novel the story of a shepherd boy who grew up in a mountain community called Kingdom Come. I was fascinated by that unusual name.

I am thinking now of a far more wonderful Kingdom Come. We are living at present in the kingdom of this world. It began with Adam and Eve in the Garden of Eden, but sin entered and wrecked that kingdom. It is still a wreck, although some of its beauty lingers. The loveliest natural scene is deceptive because underneath there is bloodshed and terror. The creatures creep about in fear; the birds look nervously in all directions; the snake glides in the grass. The reign of tooth and claw still prevails, and everything is under the curse. The earth is rent by sin and strife, by wars, and rumors of wars. We may send men to the moon, but we cannot solve the problems of earth. The kingdom of this world is a failure because the heart of man is deceitful and desperately wicked. *Science does not have the answer to sin.* So-called civilization carries the seeds of moral cancer in its heart. It will never hold out morally and spiritually to do what it hopes to do scientifically. Man is not evolving upward toward God. He started with a knowledge of God, but denied him, and has been living in rebellion ever since. He tries to build heaven without God, but his towers of Babel come crashing around his head; for "Except the Lord build the house, they labor in vain that build it" (Psalms 127:1). "The whole creation groaneth and travaileth in pain together until now" (Romans 8:22). Any man who is a citizen of this world only is a citizen of a kingdom doomed to die.

The kingdom of this world is under the power of Satan, the arch rebel who revolted against God and was cast out of heaven.

He is the prince of this world and it lies in wickedness. He does not own it, for "the earth is the Lord's and the fullness thereof" (Psalms 24:1). But he does possess it for the time being. He is a usurper, and will be thrown out one day, for the kingdoms of this world shall become the kingdom of our Lord and his Christ.

Long ago, God sent his Son to tell us about the kingdom of God. First of all, he came to deal with sin, for it was sin that wrecked the first creation. He took our sins upon him and died in our stead—as many as receive him receive power to become sons of God, members of the new race of which he is the new Adam. Here is the greatest of all race issues: whether we belong to the new race or to only the old race of sinful humanity.

The kingdom came first in the person of the King himself when Jesus lived on earth. He said, "the kingdom of God is within you" (Luke 17:21). The kingdom was embodied in the King; and when he was among us, he gave us samples of what the visible kingdom will be like when he reigns on earth. His miracles were a foretaste, an "earnest," the firstfruits of what will be regular fare in the kingdom to come. Like the spies who brought back the fruit of the promised land, our Lord gave us specimens from the age to be. When I was a boy, book salesmen offered the jackets and sample pages of certain volumes, and this prospectus was calculated to awaken an appetite for the complete book. The crumbs made you want the cake. So our Lord gave us a prospectus of that which is to be. When lepers were healed, when the blind saw, when Lazarus rose from the grave, when the poor woman in the crowd touched my Lord and was made whole—all these tasted of the powers of the world to come. When he healed the sick, it proclaimed a day coming without disease. When he raised the dead, he served notice that one day death would cease to be. When he turned water into wine, walked on water, and fed the multitude with a few loaves and fishes, he announced his sovereignty over the laws of nature. Things we now try to accomplish with tons of paraphernalia will be routine one day without cumbersome machinery. What costly equipment we must have to heal the sick or travel in space! Our Lord could be anywhere in the twinkling of an eye, and dispel disease with a touch of the hand, or enter through doors without opening them. We experiment, for instance, with devices for walking on water. Our Lord simply got out there as he was and walked on the water (not on the shore as skeptics now explain it).

So the King came and embodied the kingdom in himself with a sample case of what to expect when God's will is done on earth as in heaven.

Satan offered the kingdoms of this world to our Lord in the third temptation, but Jesus refused the shortcut and took the way of the cross. If he had accepted Satan's offer, he would have submitted to the devil. He took the Calvary road by which Satan was defeated and will be dethroned. God promised the kingdoms of this world to his Son (Psalms 2) and my Lord doesn't have to bow to the devil to get them. The devil offers the world to the Christian today, but the faithful child of God takes the way of the cross with his Lord now, and will reign with him forever. The meek shall inherit the earth. Some have said that is the only way we will ever get it, but get it we will. It will be ours because it will be his! If you want this world the way it now is, you are welcome to it! I'll take the way of the cross and bid farewell to the way of the world now. I'll wait until death is gone, and disease and dictators and the devil, when Jesus Christ takes over; then the world will belong to me and the rest of God's people. I can afford to wait.

In the meantime the kingdom is the reign of God in the hearts of men who trust Christ as Savior and obey him as Lord. It is a spiritual kingdom at present, and cometh not with observation. It is not meat and drink, but righteousness, peace, and joy in the Holy Ghost. Mind you, the righteousness comes before the peace and joy, and it is not a do-it-yourself proposition, but "in the Holy Ghost." Nobody knows how many belong to the kingdom. Statistics do not help here. Plenty of church members do not belong – only the born again, blood-washed children of God. They are a despised minority, aliens in a pagan land, pilgrims and strangers, whose citizenship is in heaven. Nowadays, when so much of this world is in the hands of the ungodly, it may not look as though we would ever rule the earth; but long ago our Savior said to a little handful of disciples who looked like they didn't have a chance: "Fear not, little flock; for it is your Father's good pleasure to give you the kingdom" (Luke 12:32).

Kingdom Come is an invisible community now. Wherever men know and serve Christ, there is the kingdom. In that sense, the kingdom has already come; but in another sense it is a coming kingdom when our Lord returns, and then it will be a visible kingdom. It is both kingdom come and kingdom coming. When we pray, "Thy kingdom come," we pray for its coming in the conversion of souls; but we also pray for its final coming when our Savior comes back to earth. Some think the kingdom is coming gradually in the conversion of the world to Christianity, and they speak of "bringing in the kingdom"; but the visible kingdom will not come until the King returns.

Not only are we now living in Kingdom Come, but it is possible to enjoy in advance some of the blessings of the kingdom that is still to come. The writer to the Hebrews speaks of those who have tasted the powers of the world to come (Hebrews 6:5). We taste these powers when we are born again, in the assurance of salvation which Fanny Crosby called "a foretaste of glory divine." We taste them in the presence of the Holy Spirit which the Scriptures call "the earnest (or first installment) of our inheritance" (Ephesians 1:14). We taste these powers when we taste the good word of God in our Bibles, when we pray, and when we enjoy the fellowship of God's people. We taste them when the Spirit that raised Jesus from the dead quickens our mortal bodies, even now before the resurrection.

> The hill of Zion yields
> A thousand sacred sweets
> Before we reach the heavenly fields,
> Or walk the golden streets.

The branches bend over the wall and we may sample some of the fruits of the age to come before we get there!

The Scriptures indicate that all the world of nature is on tiptoe, waiting for the day when the sons of God shall come into their own in a redeemed creation.

> When the beasts of the wild shall be led by a child,
> There'll be peace in the valley for me.

I never hear a woodthrush chime his vespers at the end of day but I sense a wistful longing for a better day. Dr. A. T. Roberston, dealing with Romans 8:19 wrote, "The mystical sympathy of physical nature with the work of grace is beyond the comprehension of most of us. But who can disprove it?" Goethe wrote, "Often have I had the sensation as if nature in wailing sadness entreated something of me so that not to understand what she longed for cut me to the heart." John Keble wrote;

> It was not then a poet's dream
>   An idle vaunt of song
> Such as beneath the moon's soft beam
>   On vacant fancies throng,
> Which bids me see in heaven or earth,
>   In all fair things around,
> Strong yearnings for a blest new birth
>   With sinless glories crowned.

Dr. A. J. Gordon put it this way: "The age to come is the resurrection age, the time of the redemption of the body. We know the powers of that age not simply by prediction and promise but by experience. Every miracle is a foretaste thereof, a sign of its universal healing and restitution. The driftwood and floating vegetation which met the eye of Columbus as he was keeping lookout upon his ship assured him of the proximity of the new world which he was seeking. His study of geography had assured him of the existence of that world. But now he tasted its powers, he saw and handled its actual firstfruits. So it is with us voyagers to the world to come, the millennial age, and the time of the restitution of all things. As those who have known and credited our Lord's miracles while on earth or have experienced the wonders of recovery which he has wrought as he still stretches out his hand to heal, we have tasted the powers of the coming age."

Not only does creation groan but we too long for that day

> When we shall be where we would be,
> When we shall be what we should be;
> Things that are not now nor could be
> Then shall be our own.

We can taste the powers of the coming kingdom while living in Kingdom Come! We do not have to wait for that blessed era to dawn in all its fullness. The thought of participating in it *now* exhilarates me, and I write or preach about it often. It will bear repeating! I propound no theories and am interested in no fads, but I do feel that most of us Christians are living on crackers and cheese when we might feed on the powers of the world to come before we get there, or it gets here, and to a far greater degree than we dare to experience. This is not arrived at by a complex system of thought that only scholars can comprehend, but by simple faith, and the simpler the better; faith such as the poor sick woman had when she touched my Lord in the crowd. I believe there is available strength for the body, wisdom for the mind, and power for the spirit, and that we can lay hold upon enough of everything we shall need to do all that God wants us to do, as long as he wants us to do it.

The Christian moves through the kingdom of this world as a citizen of the kingdom of God. He is not a citizen of earth trying to get to heaven, but a citizen of heaven making his way through this world. He belongs to what Peter calls "an holy nation" (1 Peter 2:9), the only Christian nation on earth, a nation within the nations. He sees everything in the light of Kingdom Come and the kingdom coming. News reports mean something entirely different from what they mean to the man of this world. Issues that excite other people leave him undisturbed. He knows there will be world peace only when the Prince of Peace returns. Projects and reforms by which unregenerate men try to legislate a better world into being mean little to him. He does not ride every bandwagon headed for the Promised Land. He pays his taxes, prays for those in authority, and favors whatever makes for as much peace and order as possible; but he does everything in the light of Kingdom Come and kingdom coming. He is a puzzle to this world; he seems detached from it and is a stranger to it.

I have read of a parade of boys in which everyone was in step except one youngster. It was discovered that under his coat he carried a transistor radio, and was marching to other music from a thousand miles away! The Christian is in step with the drumbeats of another world.

Secret orders have their passwords and codes known only to the initiated. Christians belong to the greatest of secret orders. It started with the post-resurrection appearances of our Lord limited to only his own. To this day, only God knows who belongs. He keeps the books. I invite you to join this happy band, these members of Kingdom Come, awaiting the coming kingdom.

"Thy kingdom come... For thine is the kingdom"! (Matthew 6:10, 13).

Notes of a Bugler

For if the trumpet give an uncertain sound, who shall prepare himself to the battle? (1 Corinthians 14:8).

SOME newer translations give us "bugle" instead of "trumpet." We have here the battle, the bugler, and the bugle. God's people are engaged in the greatest of all wars. "We are up against the unseen power that controls this dark world, and spiritual agents from the very headquarters of evil" (Ephesians 6:12, Phillips). Every preacher is a bugler who sounds the call to battle. The bugle is his message, and woe unto him if the notes are muffled or muted.

The battle is not going well with the church today. Too many buglers do not understand the nature of the conflict. Some are sounding retreat instead of advance, blowing taps when we need a reveille, or going left instead of straight ahead.

For over half a century I have tried to sound a clear call without any fancy notes. God did not call me to entertain the troops, but to exhort them to fight the good fight. Some time ago, a friend of mine told of listening to a speaker who spent an hour saying nothing. A lady sitting beside my friend thought it was wonderful. My friend objected, "But really he didn't say very much." "No," replied the lady, "but he implied so much!" God did not call me to preach by implication!

I have endeavored first to preach *a simple faith*. I am amazed that so many preachers are upset by new books, magazine articles, and theological fads that change from year to year like women's fashions. It is a mark of theological adolescence and spiritual immaturity to be carried about with every wind of doctrine. We dignify these fads and publicize these heresies, when they should be beneath our serious notice.

I believe the Bible is the Word of God. I am not splitting hairs over theories of inspiration. God's Word is not obsolete, it is absolute; when I accept it for what it claims to be, I have a weapon that dispels all dread, dissolves all doubt, and defeats the devil. I believe that Jesus Christ is the Son of God, that He died for my sins, rose from the dead, and is coming again. I believe that I am a son of God through faith in his only begotten Son. Josh Billings said, "I'd rather know a few things for certain than be sure of a lot of things that ain't so." I am too busy preaching God's "few things for certain" to be interested in theological beatniks and crackpot movements operating under religious auspices.

The second note which I have tried to sound is so rare that it may seem strange to include it here. I have tried to call on Christians, and especially preachers, to find time for *quiet meditation and reflection;* to be still and know God. Exercise is important, and golf has its place, although I do not play because when I find a place as pretty as a golf course I don't want to be bothered with sticks and balls. Study is indispensable, but I am not concerned just now with exercise or study, but with meditation. I grew up in the hills and spent much of my boyhood in the woods. Today, one of my greatest problems as a traveling preacher is to find outdoor solitude. City parks are not safe anymore, and I am usually stuck in a motel made for motorists, not pedestrians. Walking is my only un-American activity. When have you seen anybody just walking and thinking? A pedestrian along a highway these days is considered to be either out of his head or out of gas.

If we spent more time like our Lord, by the sea or on the mountain in meditation and prayer, we would not be so easily addled by every little theological and sociological fad that comes by. I would say to preachers: "Get alone in the woods with your Bible, away from 'the madding crowd's ignoble strife,' telephones, and committee meetings of the Sons and Daughters of I Will Arise. Read and pray until the fire burns in your bones. Forget about existentialism and demythologizes and relevance and involvement and dialogue, long enough to get the taste out of your mouth. After all, the sun shines just like it used to. The breezes blow just like they used to. The birds sing just like they used to. (I'm glad the wood thrush hasn't added any off-beat notes to his repertoire!) The Bible reads just like it used to. Come out of the woods and preach like we used to. For we sin just as we used to. We are going to heaven or hell just as we used to. And the gospel is still the power of God unto salvation and we need to be born again just as we used to. After all, *nothing important has changed.*"

Solitary meditation is a lost art. Americans cannot endure their own company. What could be worse for the average American than a rainy afternoon with TV out of order! A man came home from the office one evening lamenting: "We had a rough day; the computer broke down and everybody had to think." If anybody is lost in thought nowadays, it is because he is in unfamiliar territory.

In a day of wind, earthquake, and fire, we need to get back to Horeb and hear the still, small voice. We need some rebels in this rat race, like John the Baptist fresh from the wilderness. Paul was a city man, but even he had to go to the solitudes of Arabia to get his bearings.

In the third place, I have preached all over America that *the church must first repent.* Our Lord's last word to the church was not the great commission but "repent," and it is the last thing the church is willing to do. We hear much about revival, but revival is an Old Testament word. The New Testament word is "repent." I almost despair of our churches ever learning the difference between revival and evangelism. The average "revival" is mainly a drive for more members, and we already have too many of the kind that most of them are!

Evangelism is the preaching of the gospel in order to win the lost. Revival is a work of the Spirit among God's people, whereby they get right with God and with each other. Revival means conviction of sin among Christians, confession and forsaking of sin, restitution and reconciliation, separation from the world and obedience to God. Dr. R. A. Torrey used to say that if church members understood what revival really means, most of them would pray, "Lord, keep us from having a revival." Most church members really vote against revivals anyway by not attending them. If I were looking for most of the members of any church during a revival, I'd never go to the revival to find them.

Preaching repentance is the loneliest and most thankless business in the world. Christians go to great evangelistic gatherings where they can get lost in the crowd. Stand in a local church where everybody knows everybody and call deacons, Sunday school teachers, and choir singers to repentance, however, and you will understand what Joseph Parker meant when he said: "The man whose sermon is repentance sets himself against his age.... There is but one end for such a man: off with his head! Better not preach repentance until you have pledged your head to heaven."

The fourth note I have sounded is *the absolute lordship of Jesus Christ*. One of the greatest errors in the church today is the artificial distinction we have created between accepting Christ as Savior and confessing him as Lord. We have made two experiences of it, but the New Testament makes them one. A Christian is one who trusts Jesus as his Savior, submits to him as Lord, and takes the New Testament as the law of his life—all this should happen at the same time. Salvation is not a cafeteria line where you take what you like and leave the rest. Of course, if a man takes Jesus for all he knows him to be at that time, he is a Christian; but no man can accept Christ as Savior and wilfully refuse him as Lord, and be saved. There is no such thing as a "Come in, Savior; stay out, Lord" salvation. After all, the word "Savior" is found only twenty-four times in the New Testament, while "Lord" occurs four hundred and thirty-three times. We cannot accept his saviorhood and deny his sovereignty. What good is pardon if we still live as rebels? Salvation is free, but along with it comes discipleship, and that will cost us all we have. A believer comes to Christ; a disciple comes after him. We are long on membership these days, but short on discipleship. We hear much about stewardship; we should hear more about lordship. When Christ is Lord, stewardship will fall into line. Jesus made it clear that if we come to him, but come not after him, we cannot be his disciples (Luke 14:26, 27).

We have suffered from the preaching of cheap grace. Grace is free, but it is not cheap. People will take anything that is free, but they are not interested in discipleship. They will take Christ as Savior but not as Lord. It is high time we learned that while grace is free, it teaches us that, denying ungodliness and worldly lusts, we should live soberly, righteously, and godly in this present world as a peculiar people, zealous of good works; and that means the lordship of Christ.

The fifth note that I am sounding today is *the filling of the Holy Spirit*. Being filled with the Spirit is the duty and privilege of every Christian. Just as with making Christ Lord, it ought to begin at conversion, but it is usually a subsequent experience. Many books have been written and sermons preached about it. We argue over expressions and miss the experience. Whatever it is, most Christians don't have it. Some had rather miss a blessing than give up a prejudice. We are so afraid of getting out on a limb that we never climb the tree. For fear of too much, we make out with too little. I believe in the filling of the Spirit from the testimony of Scripture, of history, and my own experience.

A Christian is filled with the Spirit when he realizes his need, puts away all known sin, surrenders to Christ all he is and has, and by faith receives the fullness of the Spirit that he may glorify Jesus Christ in his life and testimony. Jesus told us how: "If any man thirst, let him come unto me and drink. He that believeth on me, as the scripture hath said, from within him shall flow rivers of living water" (John 7:37-38 ASV). It is a matter of thirsting, coming, drinking, believing, and overflowing.

When are we going to learn that all the wonderful things we read about in the book of Acts were simply the *outflow* and the *overflow* of the *inflow* of the Holy Spirit? If it ever happens again, it will come the same way, for "*all is vain unless* the Spirit of the Holy One come down."

Another note I seek to stress is *the church within the church*. Our Lord stands today outside Laodicea, the institutionalized modern church, saying, "If any man (anyone) hear my voice, and open the door, I will come in to him, and sup with him, and he with me" (Revelation 3:20). Rich, increased with goods and needing nothing, this vast professing church will be spewed out of his mouth as it becomes the world church, to be taken over by the world state, under Antichrist. But our Lord outside the door is gathering the assembly of the "anyones," the faithful few, the Master's minority, who will hear his voice and live in fellowship with him.

God has always been in the remnant business. Today little group movements are springing up everywhere. The idea is sound. We have been doing things the big way. It is time to do them God's little way. Gideon's first army was too large; there were too many of the kind he had for the kind of battle he was out to fight. The average church today is like a lung with pneumonia, only a few cells doing the breathing. The solution is not found by pulling out a few of the faithful to go down the street and start a new church. It does not lie in just plugging along trying to maintain the status quo, saying, "Things could be worse." Things could be better! The answer lies in starting over with a new church within the old church – the church within the church. Dr. A. J. Gordon said: "A few Spirit-filled disciples are sufficient to save a church. The Holy Spirit acting through these can and does bring recovery and health to the whole body."

One does not start a fire by kindling the backlog, but by igniting a handful of kindling wood. I am gathering a little kindling wood wherever I go, to start fires in the churches. To change the figure, I believe that the mainstream of God's purpose is moving today, not in sluggish institutional Christianity but in this church within the church, not in the extensive but in the intensive, not in smug Laodicea but in the "anyones" who will hear the Savior's voice and open the door.

I have emphasized another note, an unfamiliar note but none the less important: *the need for a New Testament prophet.* We have pastors, teachers, and evangelists in abundance; but we need some prophets, not foretellers but forth-tellers, who speak for

God to the church and the nation. We need the voice of a John the Baptist in the modern wilderness; a Micaiah who, when four hundred false prophets bid Ahab go up against Ramoth Gilead, says, "what the Lord saith unto me, that will I speak" (1 Kings 22:14). Joseph Parker said, "The world hates the four hundred and first prophet."

The prophet is a "square," an odd number in a standardized, regimented, collectivized society. He walks alone, is not popular at clubs and luncheons, and has little regard for forms and ceremonies. Amos was not chummy with Jeroboam II, nor did he hobnob with Amaziah at Bethel. John the Baptist was not a guest in Herod's palace; he was a prisoner in Herod's jail. The prophet is not a diplomat. He is not out to arrange a compromise, but to deliver an ultimatum. He has not read, *How to Win Friends and Influence People.* He is not a reed shaken by the wind, nor is he garbed in soft clothing. He is lean and hungry, and a little angry. He prefers being a lean bird in the woods to a fat bird in a cage. Organized religion hates him but cannot control him. His contemporaries stone him, and the next generation builds a monument in his honor. Of all kinds of preachers, he is needed most and wanted least. Like Jehoshaphat, we may well enquire today: "Is there not here a prophet of the Lord besides, that we might enquire of him?" (2 Chronicles 18:6).

Finally, I would declare with no uncertain sound that *Jesus is coming to earth again.* The church missed the road long ago when she stopped looking for the King to come back, and started building the kingdom here. There is indeed a spiritual kingdom: the reign of God in the hearts of men—not meat and drink, but righteousness, peace, and joy in the Holy Ghost. The visible kingdom will not be brought in by education, reformation, or legislation. The King will set it up when he returns. That will be the great society! If we understood that, misguided souls would not be riding all kinds of queer bandwagons bound for the promised land, trying to bring in a counterfeit millennium and superimpose a false kingdom of heaven, a profane Paradise, on an unregenerate society.

I believe that this present world order will end in a world church and world state under Antichrist. I believe that my Lord will come back to reign on this earth. I believe in the final redemption of nature, when the lion and lamb shall lie down together.

> The beasts of the wild shall be led by a child;
> There'll be peace in the valley some day.

I live in the present spiritual kingdom while I wait for the coming visible kingdom. I live in kingdom come while I wait for the coming kingdom. It is possible to taste the powers of the age to come before it arrives!

The world is waiting for the sunrise; the whole creation is on tiptoe awaiting the manifestation of the sons of God. I am not waiting for something to happen; I am looking for Someone to come! I can't understand why some Christians say, "O yes, of course I believe in the second coming of Christ," but never seem thrilled over the prospect. They act as though it didn't matter and seem embarrassed when it is mentioned. If I know anything about the grace of God, it teaches us to live soberly, righteously, and godly, looking for that blessed hope, and I want to spend my days learning, living, and looking. Before the great trumpet sounds, I want to sound the bugle call clearly, for if the bugler sounds the bugle uncertainly, who shall prepare himself for the battle?

Revival at Shechem

IN the last chapter of Joshua, Israel's great leader gathers the people together for a farewell message and a call to revival. They are now in the promised land but living in that perilous state known as peace without victory. They have not driven out the inhabitants of the land and now they are in danger of being engulfed by the idolatry around them. They had grown tired of fighting and had settled for peaceful coexistence, but it did not work then any more than it works today with Communism. There is no substitute for victory. There is only the alternative: defeat.

> They ensnare their children's children
> Who make compromise with sin.

Joshua began his message with a rundown of past blessings; then he called upon the people to renounce their idols and serve the Lord—a negative and positive exhortation. He knew the weakness of Israel. Abraham had been called out of idolatry, and the seeds of that evil lay dormant ready to spring into weeds of outright apostasy. The people still possessed household images such as Rachel stole from Laban. He remembered how even at Sinai they had promised to serve God, only to worship a golden calf six weeks later. So deeply ingrained was this evil propensity that he met it head on.

Any genuine revival must begin with the renouncing of strange gods. There is as much idolatry in our churches as there was in Israel. The love of money (1 Timothy 6:10), our lower natures (Philippians 3:17-21), pleasure (2 Timothy 3:4), our own selves (2 Timothy 3:2); all these are false gods we serve today. John's first epistle closes with the words, "Little children, keep yourselves from idols." Real revival begins when Christians pray:

> Lord Jesus, I long to be perfectly whole;
> I want thee forever to live in my soul,
> *Break down every idol,* cast out every foe;
> Now wash me, and I shall be whiter than snow.

Charles G. Finney says that revival is "a new beginning of obedience to God" and that obedience is both negative and positive, renouncing idols and saying with Joshua: "As for me and my house, we will serve the Lord" (Joshua 24:15). Somebody must start a revival; Joshua began with himself and so should every pastor. Our Lord's letters to the churches in Asia, calling for repentance and revival, were addressed to the angel—the pastor of the church.

The people responded, "God forbid that we should forsake the Lord, to serve other gods.... Therefore will we also serve the Lord for he is our God (v. 16, 18). It sounded good, but Joshua sensed superficiality and unreality in it. Their dedication was too glib and shallow. He answered, "Ye cannot serve the Lord" (v. 19). Instead of encouraging their vows of allegiance, he threw cold water on them. What strange procedure is this? Should he not have nourished such weak affirmations in the hope that they would grow stronger? *It is scriptural to challenge cheap dedication.* McLaren says: "The best way to deepen and confirm good resolutions too-swiftly formed is to state very plainly the difficulty of keeping them."

I have been much exercised about this matter in my own ministry. I have seen crowds promise God their full devotions on a Sunday night in special meetings, only to find them missing by Friday night's ball game! Such people do not mean business. They are like these Israelites of old whom we are now studying, and of whom the Psalmist wrote: "Nevertheless they did flatter him with their mouth, and they lied unto him with their tongues. For their heart was not right with him, neither were they stedfast in his covenant" (Psalms 78:36, 37). We do such people a great wrong when we accept superficial dedication, for it confirms them in their hypocrisy and leads them to mistake the false for the real, deceiving themselves. It would be better if they made no profession at all.

We are afraid to take Joshua's position today for fear of scaring away prospective church members. It was exactly the attitude of our Lord in this matter. He had something to say about superficial dedications. He spoke of the son who said, "I go, Sir," and went not. He spoke of those who receive the word with joy, but have no roots in themselves. He answered three prospective disciples with his stern word about the foxes and the birds, letting the dead bury their dead, and looking back after putting one's hand to the plow. He sobered the enthusiasm of a multitude with three "cannot's" of discipleship (Luke 14:25-33). He let the rich young ruler go away sorrowful rather than be a cheap follower.

We suffer today from "cheap grace." Dietrich Bonhoeffer says that after Luther, Germany became Christian and Lutheran, but at the cost of true discipleship. Our Lord does not cast out those who come to him, but they must mean business; after coming to him, they must come after him. Coming to him we receive rest, but as we learn of him we find rest. It is easy to become a Christian, for the gift of God is eternal life; in another sense it is difficult to be a Christian, because it costs us ourselves—all we are and have. Our Lord said that if we come to him but do not come after him, we cannot be his disciples (Luke 14:26-27). Grace is God's unmerited favor but that grace teaches us to deny ungodliness and worldly lusts, and to live soberly, righteously and godly in this present world.

Joshua reminded the people that God is a holy and jealous God. We are not going to have a revival until people see God in his holiness—a God who will not look upon sin, and a jealous God who will not share his throne in our hearts with another. Until we face up to that, we cannot serve the Lord.

There was another revival at this same Shechem long before the days of Joshua. Jacob had wandered from Bethel to Shechem where Dinah, his daughter, got into trouble. His sons took vengeance on the Shechemites and Jacob was sore distressed. Then God commanded him to return to Bethel and dwell there and make an altar unto the Lord. We live at Shechem today, the place of broken vows, broken homes and broken hearts; we need to return to Bethel. Jacob obeyed promptly, ordered his household to put away their strange gods, change their garments, and return to the place of blessing. Like Joshua, as for him and his house he would serve the Lord. Like Joshua, he was the head of the house. He did not ask his household whether or not they wanted to go, nor was he afraid of frustrating Junior; he simply announced that they were returning to Bethel. More fathers like that in America today would answer a good many problems of broken homes and wayward youngsters.

The family obeyed, giving up their strange gods and earrings which Jacob buried under an oak. If American churches followed a similar procedure, we would fill all the national forests in the country with surrendered idols! Paul had a book burning at Ephesus, and Savonarola witnessed a similar sight in Florence. There was considerable joking sometime ago, when members of a certain sect made a bonfire of worldly trinkets: tobacco, evil books, and other miscellaneous items not consistent with godly living. It is no laughing matter. We might well check our own premises and see what we have to contribute to a holy bonfire.

We need also to change our garments. There are a few like those saints in Sardis who have not defiled their garments, but too many wear the filthy rags of self-righteousness, the spotted garments of worldliness, or the gray garments of compromise. The prodigal was received by the father just as he was, but he had to put on a new robe for fellowship, and so must we.

We read that Jacob and his company journeyed, and the terror of the Lord accompanied them. God's presence and power are with the man who is headed for Bethel—who has decided that he and his house will serve the Lord. When they arrived at Bethel, Jacob renamed it "El-beth-el": the God of the house of God. God had become more important than any place.

> Once earthly joy I craved;
> Sought peace and rest;
> Now thee alone I seek,
> Give what is best.

This is true revival, deep and definite. We are living at Shechem. It is not enough to make cheap dedication. Our God is holy and jealous. Let us confess and forsake sin. Let us give up our strange gods and change our garments. Let us be on our way in the path of obedience, and the terror of the Lord will attend us.

The Only Christian Nation

But ye are a chosen generation, a royal priesthood, an holy nation, a peculiar people; that ye should show forth the praises of him who hath called you out of darkness into his marvelous light (1 Peter 2:9).

ONE of the institutions fast disappearing from American life is the old-fashioned Fourth of July celebration, with its speeches about our national heritage extolling the heroes of our illustrious past. The greatest Fourth of July celebration is now held in Denmark, three thousand five hundred miles away. For years our national heroes have been debunked and their reputations riddled by muckrakers, until our children regard them, not with admiration, but with cynicism. Subtle international influences have encouraged reducing these giants to insignificance. They had their faults, of course, but any generation that has failed as miserably as we have today has no business ridiculing its forefathers. We need a good dose of old-fashioned Americanism.

Recently I visited the home of Theodore Roosevelt. It took me back to a period now strangely remote. If there is such a thing as turning over in one's grave, the Colonel must be in a constant whirl! I remembered his words: "The professed internationalist usually sneers at nationalism, patriotism, what we call Americanism. He bids us forswear our love of country in the name of the world at large. We nationalists answer, he has begun at the wrong end. As the world now is, it is only the man who ardently loves his country first who in actual practice can help any country at all." Certainly, a man is a better member of the human family if his first loyalty is to his own, and a better member of the family of nations if he is true first to his native land.

I heard General Douglas MacArthur say on his seventy-fifth birthday: "Seductive murmurs are arising that we are provincial and immature, or reactionary and stupid, when we idealize our own country; that there is a higher destiny for us under another more general flag. Repudiate them in the marketplace, from the platform, and the pulpit." We need to recover American nationalism. I do not mean isolationism. We should always be ready to cooperate with fellow nations for the common good, but not amalgamate at the cost of the characteristics that made us great.

Our text sets forth another kind of nationalism. America is not a Christian nation. There is only one Christian nation—God's people, the church of Jesus Christ. There are Christians in all nations, but only one Christian nation: the fellowship of believers, a nation within the nations. The world is not being converted, and never will be. God is taking out a people for his name. Christians are *colonials,* for our citizenship is in heaven; we are a colony of heaven on earth (Philippians 3:20). We are also *nationals,* for we belong to the "holy nation" of our text. We are also "a peculiar people," which does not mean that we are queer (although some are!) but that we are God's purchased people, bought with the blood of our Lord. We should not be queer, but we ought to be different. And yet Phillips puts it this way: "Indeed your former companions may think it very *queer* that you will no longer join with them in their riotous excesses, and accordingly say all sorts of unpleasant things about you" (1 Peter 4:4).

Today, we face the same dangers in the church that we confront as a nation. Just as America is in danger of losing her national identity in a world state, so Christians may lose their spiritual identity in a world church. There are those who would downgrade America and whittle away the Constitution. Some of us are still satisfied with this country. It is the only one people are trying to get into! They are trying to get out of Cuba, East Germany, Hungary, China, and many another land. I would be glad to embark all beatniks who like some other system better, and wave them goodbye out of New York (or any other port) as far as I could see them. By the same token, there are those who downgrade Christianity and deny the Scriptures. Some even affirm that God is dead and the church defunct, and that we ought to close the churches and get out into the world speaking a new language—the lingo of the times.

This is not the America I knew as a boy; nor is this merely old-age nostalgia, for younger Americans like Paul Harvey lament, "I never left the old country, the old country left me." Nor is the church today the church I used to know. Nations run their courses and so do churches. America still has within her the possibility of renewal; and the church, by the grace of God, still holds the possibility of revival. What the country needs is a new breed of Americans, and what the church needs is a new breed of Christians to counteract phony Americans and counterfeit Christians, who are a disgrace to both nation and church.

I am an American by birth and by choice. I was born an American, but some who were born here seem to prefer some other heritage. I choose America: the Declaration of Independence and the Constitution of the United States in their original forms, before we started tampering with them. I choose America: her rocks and rills, her woods and templed hills. My heart still skips a beat when the flag goes by. If that is provincial, I am glad to be a "back number." I am a Christian by birth and by choice: by birth, because I was born a second time into the kingdom of God; by choice, because I choose Jesus. I know that God chose me before I chose him, but still he says, "choose you this day whom ye will serve" (Joshua 24:15). Patrick Henry said: "As for me, give me liberty or give me death." Joshua said, "As for me and my house, we will serve the Lord." I choose to stand with that red-headed Virginian as an American, and with that gallant old soldier as a servant of God. I choose the Bible, the Constitution of the holy nation, in its original form, before the demythologizers started tampering with it. What they call myth I call miracle; what they call fable I call fact. I can still endure sound doctrine. I do not have itching ears, and need no false teacher to tickle them!

But why are Christians "an holy nation"? Certainly not to sit in self-righteous isolation. That was the curse of Pharisaism. Our text tells us: "That ye should shew forth the praises of him who hath called you out of darkness into his marvelous light." Communism shows forth the praises of Karl Marx. Communism does not say that some other way is just as good. Christians are ambassadors for Christ. Every citizen of this holy nation is an ambassador. An American ambassador is not out to make Americans of everybody, but a Christian ought to be out to make Christians of everybody. It has been said that Communism is out to win the world, but that Americans are out to enjoy it. Communism is not out to win more territory, but to capture the souls of men. The greatest soul-winners today are Communists winning men for the devil. Dr. Malik said: "The Russians are utterly devoted to their cause. That is not true of most Americans I know. Why do you in America not pay the price? Why do you not press the battle to victory with the weapon God has given you, the heritage of the Christian faith?" Whitaker Chambers said: "Communism is no stronger than the failure of other faiths."

We need to be what we are as Christians—an holy nation, Christian colonials, heavenly nationals, a Master's minority in a pagan world, a spearhead of expendables willing to spend and be spent—showing forth the excellencies of our Lord. This is the only Christian nation. We belong to it only by being born into it through faith in Jesus Christ. We cannot take out naturalization papers! And every citizen of this nation is an ambassador. If we are not ambassadors we are traitors. Which are you?

Freedom Through Faith That Follows

THE words of our Lord, "Ye shall know the truth, and the truth shall make you free" (John 8:32), have long been a favorite with makers of banners, slogans, inscriptions, and graduating sermons. Actually, this illustrates the folly of lifting a text out of its context in order to make a pretext. Taken as they stand, these words could mean anything to anybody. The verse raises two stupendous questions: what is truth? and what is freedom? It presents two tremendous issues: how to know the truth, and how to be free. It sets forth two pursuits that have engaged humanity more than any other: the search for truth, and the quest for freedom. Every school building, every scientific laboratory, every house of worship speaks of man's search for truth. All the present worldwide turmoil, with new nations being born every few days, testifies to man's quest for freedom.

Without its context, the text does not answer the questions it raises. As usually quoted, it leaves out the first word, "And." That means something has gone before. What has gone before is this: "If ye continue in my word, then are ye my disciples indeed." The next verse follows naturally: *"And* ye shall know the truth, and the truth shall make you free." But even that is not enough. If we continue, there must have been a time when we started. If we abide, there must be a time when we took up residence. So, we read first that these words were spoken to "those Jews which *believed* on him." Putting these three verses in order, we have this sequence: we believe; we become disciples; we continue in the word; we know the truth; we are made free. Here is the secret of truth and freedom, freedom through faith that follows. The way to freedom is to believe on Jesus Christ, become his disciple, and continue in his word.

Here lies the tragedy in most of the professing church today. Most of our church members know nothing of spiritual freedom, and it is because they are not true believers, or else they are not following disciples. We are long on membership but short on discipleship. We are more anxious to gather statistics than to grow saints. The sheep hear the Shepherd's voice and they follow him. The knowledge that sets men free does not lie in mere mental acceptance of a proposition, but in heart obedience to a Person. We dare not mention the cost of discipleship to a church prospect lest we frighten him away. The Christian life, the way of the cross, calls for discipline, and nobody wants discipline. Training in self-denial, preparation of body, mind, and spirit to be soldiers of the cross is very unpopular business nowadays. Call church members to that and they will rebel as our Lord's hearers did when this text was first spoken. They are willing to be professed believers but not practicing disciples.

Certainly one does not become an athlete without discipline. Don Ameche says that when acrobats are not performing they are practicing. Ask a great pianist how many hours he practices! Heifetz recently complained that modern violin students do not know much about discipline. Men exercise great self-denial to win corruptible crowns, but the church is fighting the greatest battle of all time with the most undisciplined army on the face of the earth. When we observe the slovenly living of most professed Christians, we do not wonder that we make little impact on our day and generation.

How can we expect to be advanced students in the school of Christ if we are satisfied to be babes in kindergarten? The dropout percentage is higher here than in any other school on earth. Few make the honor roll, few care to graduate from this life *cum laude* with the Master's "Well done."

The saints of old put everything they had into it. They made the Christian life their business. They strove to enter in at the straight gate. They labored to enter into rest. They gave diligence to make their calling and election sure. The kingdom of God was their absorbing passion—their meat and drink. They believed;

they continued in the Word; they were disciples; they knew the truth, and they were set free.

> They climbed the steep ascent of heaven
> Through peril, toil and pain.
> O God, may grace to us be given
> To follow in their train!

"I Have Set My Face"

"FOR the Lord God will help me; therefore shall I not be confounded: therefore have I set my face like a flint, and I know that I shall not be ashamed" (Isaiah 50:7). So wrote Isaiah concerning God's suffering servant, and when that suffering servant came to earth "he stedfastly set his face to go to Jerusalem" (Luke 9:51). Our Lord did not have a hard face, for it was full of love and compassion; but he did have a set face. He had made up his mind. He knew where he was going. He had fixed his course and he allowed no one to deflect him. The devil offered him the kingdoms of this world but our Savior took no shortcut; he chose the way of Calvary. John the Baptist in prison questioned whether Jesus was "he that should come" (Luke 7:19), but our Lord answered, in effect, "I'm running on schedule and doing what I came to do." His brothers urged him to go up to Jerusalem and perform before the world. That was not his program. Peter confessed Christ but denied the cross and remonstrated at the thought of Calvary. Our Lord declared him to be speaking not for God but for the devil. When he heard of Herod's threats, he called the king a fox and made it clear that he would go ahead with his plans as scheduled. He had set his face like a flint, and neither friend nor foe, man nor devil, could divert him from his goal.

Throughout the Word of God, the heroes of faith were men who set their faces like a flint. Caleb "wholly followed the Lord God" (Joshua 14:14). Joshua said, "As for me and my house, we will serve the Lord." Elijah asked, "How long halt ye between two opinions?" (1 Kings 18:21). Daniel "purposed in his heart" (Daniel 1:8) to be true to God. Paul said: "this one thing I do" (Philippians 3:13). He also set his face to go to Jerusalem and said, "none of these things move me" (Acts 21:24).

One of our biggest problems today is that most of our church people have never really made up their minds to follow Jesus Christ. They are like Mr. Looking-both-ways in *The Pilgrims Progress,* or like Lot's wife looking back toward Sodom. They are like the man in the Civil War who wore a blue coat and gray trousers and was shot at from both sides. They are like a donkey between two bales of hay—undecided as to which to eat. They are like the son in our Lord's parable who said, "I go, Sir" (Matthew 22:30), and went not. They receive the word with joy, but have no root nor depth and soon fall away. They never really make up their minds, and are like the man who was asked, "Do you have trouble making decisions?" He replied, "Yes and no."

In the ninth chapter of Luke we read that our Lord stedfastly set His face to go to Jerusalem. In the same chapter, we read in contrast of three who were exactly opposite; they were not really going anywhere. They sounded as though they were serious, but one had not counted the cost, one wanted to bury his father, and another to bid his family goodbye before following Jesus. Whether it be the uncounted cost, the unburied corpse, or the unforsaken circle, their attitude was, "I will follow Thee BUT...." Our Lord made it very clear to each of them that he meant business, that he was going somewhere, and that his kingdom was no place for a man with his face pointed in one direction and his feet in the other.

I have been a pastor and have tried everything to induce church members to go on with God. I have scolded, praised, coaxed, and persuaded; but I am convinced that they go where they want to go, and where their hearts are, their heels will follow. We are dealing largely with a mixed multitude of uncommitted, disinterested, undisciplined people who have never set their faces to say, "This one thing I do." Theirs is the sin of dissipated devotion. As someone has put it, their lives are not like swords with one point, but like brooms ending in a thousand straws.

Dr. J. B. Gambrell was a great dog lover as a boy. He got hold of a book that told him what he could be in life if he applied himself. He decided, "I cannot be what I ought and keep up with all these dogs," so he gave up dogs. He once wrote quite a piece about the neighborhood dog that wears no collar, is unattached, doesn't belong to anybody, feels no responsibility to keep stray dogs and cats off any place, goes around smiling and wagging his tail, and will bark as much at one house as another. The neighborhood dog, Gambrell wrote, is broad-minded, makes up with everybody, gets in no fights, for to him nothing is worth fighting for. "Judicious barking", we read further, "is a fine trait, but miscellaneous barking is worth nothing, and is confusing to dogs that are really hunting something." Then Dr. Gambrell made his application. "The neighborhood dog has a lot of kin who are too broad-minded to join any church. They run to all churches, particularly if there is a special service, for they like crowds. The man who says one church is as good as another doesn't love any church enough to be of any use to it. There are hoboes in the dog world and deadbeats in the religious world. A thousand of them would never support a church or send a missionary."

These are the opposite of the saints of the set face! When Cortez landed on these shores, he burned his ships so that he and his company could not leave. He made no arrangements for a retreat. He had come to stay. God grant us a crop of saints who have stedfastly set their faces to go to Jerusalem; who will allow neither man nor the devil, friend nor foe, to deflect them from their holy resolve, "This one thing I do!"

The Christian and This World

SERMONS on worldliness are rare these days. The new word is "secularism." Billy Sunday used to say that the term "worldly Christian" was a misnomer. Of course, Billy didn't put it that way. He said, "You might as well talk about a heavenly devil!" That is in line with the New Testament definition that the friend of the world is the enemy of God.

I am convinced that many people we call worldly Christians are not Christians at all. Our Savior said, "My sheep hear my voice ... and they follow me" (John 10:27). A sheep may fall into a mudhole but is not satisfied to stay there. A hog is at home in a mudhole, and Peter tells us that false teachers who revert to their evil ways belong in that category.

It is true that we are not to judge people. "The Lord knoweth them that are his" (2 Timothy 2:19), and I am glad that he does, otherwise some of them would be pretty hard to identify! That same verse goes on to declare that all who claim to be the Lord's should depart from iniquity. When I see a bird that looks like a duck, quacks like a duck, paddles in the water like a duck, and prefers the company of ducks, I conclude that it must be a duck. "Birds of a feather flock together," and where we feel most at home is where we belong. "We know that we have passed from death unto life, because we love the brethren" (John 3:14). If we do not enjoy being with the brethren, certain conclusions are in order. When Peter and John were let go, we read that they went to their own company. Where do you go when you are let go? I'd hate to track down some church members when they get several hundred miles away from home. When Peter got out of jail, he headed for a prayer meeting. We gravitate to what lures us most and eventually show up where, at heart, we belong.

The world that God so loved that he gave his Son is the world of lost souls, and we ought to love lost souls. It was Dr. Candlish who said: "If we loved this world as God loved it we would not love it as we shouldn't love it." When God's Word says, "Love not the world" (John 2:15), it means this present age and set-up which is under the devil, the god of this age, and the prince of this world. The whole world lies in wickedness. Our Lord came to deliver us from this present evil world (Galatians 3:4). Before we were saved, we walked according to the course of this world (Ephesians 2:2), but after we are saved we head in another direction.

John has more to say about the world than any other New Testament writer. In our Lord's high-priestly prayer, in the seventeenth chapter of John, he forever locates us as believers with regard to this age. First, he says we have been saved *out of the world* (v. 6). We are the called-out ones. We have been saved out of this world system and given a new position with Christ in the heavenlies. Our citizenship is in heaven, and our standing up there and our state down here, our position up there and our condition down here ought to match. We are pilgrims and strangers, exiles and aliens, and this world is our passage but not our portion, as Matthew Henry said long ago. The Scriptures tell us, "this is not your rest" (Micah 2:10), and "here have we no continuing city" (Hebrews 13:14). A dog is at home in this world, for this is the only world a dog will ever know; but we cannot make ourselves at home here, for we were made for another world.

Our Lord said furthermore that we are *in the world* (verse 11). Although we have been saved out of it, we still have to live in its houses, trade in its stores, and mix with its people. The old mystics tried to make themselves holier by hiding from society, but living in a hole does not make you holier! Indeed, Paul wrote that to avoid company-ing with evil men, we would have to leave this world (1 Corinthians 5:10). Our Lord prayed in this same high priestly prayer: "I pray not that thou shouldest take them out of the world, but that thou shouldest keep them from the evil" (verse 15). He was in the world, and was not a recluse nor a hermit. He went to weddings, and was called a friend of publicans and sinners. Where cross the crowded ways of men, he could be found. He was criticized by the Pharisees who were separated from sinners but not from sin. He associated with the world, but had no fellowship with it.

He says further, *they are not of the world* (verses 14, 16). This is so important that he repeats it. When the boat is in the water, that is one matter; when the water is in the boat, that is something else. We are not to be conformed to this world (Romans 12:2); we are to keep ourselves unspotted from the world (James 1127); we are to have no fellowship with the unfruitful works of darkness (Ephesians 5:11). We are not to love the world, neither the things that are in the world (1 John 2:15). We are to deny ungodliness and the lusts of this age (Titus 2:12). This imposing world set-up with its pagan culture is no friend of grace to help us on to God. We cannot serve two masters. Alexander MacLaren said: "The measure of our discord with the world is the measure of our accord with Christ." Gypsy Smith said: "If you are in with God, you are at outs with this world." Dr. G. Campbell Morgan said: "The world hates Christian people, that is, if they see Christ in them. The measure in which the world agrees with us and says we are really a fine type of Christian, we are so entirely broad, is the measure in which we are unlike Christ."

Our Lord said to his brothers: "The world cannot hate you; but me it hateth, because I testify of it, that the works thereof are evil" (John 7:7). He said to his disciples: "If the world hate you, ye know that it hated me before it hated you. If ye were of the world, the world would love his own: but because ye are not of the world, but I have chosen you out of the world, therefore the world hateth you" (John 15:18, 19). Put all of this together and we have this: the world cannot hate its own, but it hates Jesus Christ and will hate his true disciples. "The world knoweth us not, because it knew him not" (1 John 3:1). All of these verses from John ought to settle forever the status of the Christian in this world.

The Savior said one thing more in his prayer concerning this matter: "As Thou hast sent me into the world, even so have I also sent them *into the world*" (Verse 18). Here, then, is the summing up of the Christian's relation to this world as set forth in our Lord's prayer. We have been saved *out of the world*; we still must live *in the world*; we are not *of the world*; we have been saved to go back *into the world* to win others out of it, and that is the only business we have in the world! We are not to sit in judgment on the age. We are the salt of the earth and the light of the world, and, as our Lord said in this same prayer (verse 19), for their sakes we should sanctify ourselves—be set apart—to minister to the need of this age.

The Way of the Cross Leads Home is a familiar old song. Everybody would agree to the first verse, that there is no other way, but we are not so agreed on the last verse:

> Then I bid farewell to the way of the world,
> To walk in it nevermore.

It is quite evident that we cannot walk two ways at once. There is only one song for the Christian on this point:

> The world behind me, the cross before me,
> No turning back, no turning back.

Earthquakes

OUR Lord told us that among the disturbances preceding his return would be earthquakes. We are having our share of them nowadays, not only physical, but other varieties not recorded on seismographs. Political, social, and religious earthquakes are convulsing the world. Humanity is in ferment. Crime, violence, lawlessness, bloodshed, perversion, riots, wars and rumors of wars—every continent trembles in world upheaval. Even the religious world reels and rocks, and Roman Catholicism itself is in commotion.

Most of the earthquakes shaking the world today are not the works of God. Satan is the prince of this age, and these convulsions are the mystery of lawlessness boiling to its climax under Antichrist. We had a major earthquake in 1917, when communism started an upheaval that has kept the world in turmoil ever since. The earth trembles in anarchy. City streets are no longer safe. Humanity has gone sex crazy. Perversion eats like a cancer. Wild maniacs pose as leaders. Howling mobs show up on every news report. A crowd of students was asked recently, "Why are you demonstrating?" They replied, "Isn't everybody?"

We live in a scientific revolution. Man has become self-sufficient in his technological know-how and has given God his walking papers. We no longer consider the heavens and ask in humility, "What is man?" We consider man and say proudly, "What are the moon and the stars?" God has been humanized and man deified. We expect God to wait on us like a celestial flunkey. The new angle is that the church is the servant of man. But we serve men because we first serve God. Apart from that, we have only humanism and humanitarian-ism.

Recently, I read a magazine article describing the church of the future. I could say only, "Thank God, I won't be here to see it!"

Ecumenism is another earthquake. Rome is abandoning some of her ritual and Protestantism is adding to hers. A modified Romanism and an apostate Protestantism merge into a colossal world church. That will be the church of the future, but it will not be a New Testament church. It will be the harlot riding the beast.

New Testament Christianity began with a series of earthquakes. We need to meet today's world revolutions with the power that shook the world almost twenty centuries ago. The apostolic age holds the answer to the atomic age. We must meet the "demon-stration" of the powers of darkness with a demonstration of the Holy Spirit.

When the Savior died on Calvary there was an earthquake (Matthew 27:51). When he rose from the dead a few days later, there was another earthquake (Matthew 28:2). Christ died for our sins—and there was an earthquake. Christ rose for our justification—and there was another earthquake.

Do I believe these were literal earthquakes? I do. If this were just a martyr dying for a cause, merely an example of self-sacrifice, no. But if God invaded history and visited earth; if the only-begotten Son of God who had no sin in him took all sin on him, and settled for time and eternity the greatest of all problems that includes all other problems—then I have no trouble believing that the greatest double event in all history included two earthquakes.

> Well might the sun in darkness hide
> And shut his glories in,
> When Christ the mighty Maker died
> For man the creature's sin.

Isaac Watts had no difficulty with earthquakes at Calvary and the open tomb!

Not only did the gospel begin with earthquakes, so did the church. In the fourth chapter of Acts we read that Peter and John were forbidden to preach. They returned to the Christian company and everybody went to prayer. They reminded God of his words in the second Psalm and prayed, "Grant unto thy servants that with all boldness they may speak thy word" (Acts 4:29). The word "boldness" is found three times in this chapter. The rulers, "when they saw the boldness of Peter and John ... took knowledge of them, that they had been with Jesus" (v. 13). The church prayed for boldness (v. 29). Then came the earthquake, the place was shaken, they were filled with the Spirit and spoke the word of God with boldness (v. 31). Boldness was seen by the world, sought by the church, and supplied by the Spirit.

Was this a literal earthquake? Certainly. God was in the earth-shaking business and these early Christians were in partnership with God. They faced a crisis. They might have decided, "After all, maybe we have been going at things too dangerously. There is no point in sticking our necks out. We had better go in for peaceful coexistence." If they had toned down their enthusiasm and soft-pedaled their testimony, Christianity would have died of dry rot and the gospel would have perished from the earth. Instead, they asked for more boldness—the very thing that got them into trouble the first time!

We are at another crossroads. No question is of greater moment than this: shall we let the hostility of this world scare us into becoming diplomats on good terms with the world, the flesh, and the devil, instead of flaming witnesses in a head-on collision with a godless age? These early Christians stirred up the devil. Our best endeavors today are met by a polite yawn. We need to stop passing resolutions and begin promoting revolutions with prayer meetings that end in earthquakes.

The Quakers got their name from the fact that they quaked under the power of God. They were shaken by what they believed. Too many today are shaky about what they believe! The only shaking that some churches know is the commotion in the recreation building. If the emphasis on re-creation kept pace with the emphasis on recreation, the sanctuary might shake once more. Some of our mausoleums haven't had a tremor in fifty years.

We are the salt of the earth, but too much of the salt is content to repose in saltcellars playing church on Sunday morning, when it needs to be shaken out of its smug complacency into the carcass of a putrefying society. We are not meant to be salt depositories but salt dispensers. We need a shaking such as the Jerusalem church had when persecution scattered it in all directions. We are not going to have a spiritual earthquake in the world until we have one in the church, and we will not have one in the church until we recognize the crisis and pray in holy desperation until the place is shaken.

There was another earthquake in Philippi. When Paul visited that city, a demonized girl proclaimed his presence as a servant of God showing the way of salvation. She announced the gospel but did not accept it. It was a testimony of lip, not of life, and Paul did not accept the witness of the devil any more than did our Lord when Satan recognized him as the Holy One of God. Jesus Christ does not want patronage; he demands absolute submission. How different from those today who say truth is truth, no matter who says it, and who welcome the endorsement of the devil!

When the demonized girl was converted, her masters rose in anger. Paul and Silas were beaten and jailed, but they sang and prayed and God sent an earthquake. When the gospel hurts the devil's business, trouble begins. When the demon-possessed hogs of Gadara drowned themselves, their owners were aroused. When Paul's preaching in Ephesus turned people from idols to God, the image makers started an uproar. There is something wrong when the church can exist in the community without protest from the hog owners and image makers of iniquity. Paul did not lecture on demonism in Philippi. He preached the gospel, but when people really believe the gospel they stop patronizing the devil. Every time Paul won a convert, the devil lost a customer! Too many join church nowadays and go right on doing business with the temples of evil. We are not stirring an uproar from the devil's business because he still has our business. Too many converts of the church are still customers of Satan. If the church ever recovers the power to break up demonism in the world around it, it will bring down the wrath of the devil and the persecution of the devil's crowd, but we will learn how to sing in prison and pray down earthquakes.

Will the church go underground? It might develop more power underground than it is manifesting above ground these days. After all, it was the Christians in the catacombs who put the Romans in the Colosseum out of business! We are not going to pray down earthquakes at committee meetings in church basements sipping coffee and listening to the minutes of the last meeting. We are heirs to a movement that started with earthquakes. We are not going to shake the world until the gospel that shook our forefathers shakes us. Christ died and rose to the accompaniment of an earthquake. We must believe and preach that gospel with a power that shakes prayer meetings, that brings down the wrath of evil, that sings at midnight in dungeons, that opens prison doors and that converts jailers. This is no time to be shaky about it. It is high time to be shaken by it.

Let me remind you that the Lamb of God who died in an earthquake is not through with this world. He is coming again. There will be a final earthquake when every mountain and island shall move out of its place. The kings of the earth and the great men and the rich men and the chief captains and the mighty men and every bondman and every free man shall hide in the dens and in the rocks of the mountains. They will call on rocks and mountains to fall on them and hide them from the face of him that sitteth on the throne and from the wrath of the Lamb—for the great day of his wrath will have come, and who shall be able to stand? We are living between the earthquake of grace and the earthquake of glory. An old lady said, during an earthquake when everybody else was terrified, "I'm glad I've got a God who can shake this world like that!" He has done it and will do it again. He can do it now. Thank God for a faith that shakes the world!

Like Him in This World

As he is, so are we in this world (1 John 4:17).

OF all the New Testament writers, John stated the greatest truths in simplest terms. He clothed profundity with simplicity. As it stands in our King James Version, he spoke mainly in monosyllables. Our text is a fair sample. "As he is, so are we in this world." You cannot say that in shorter words. You cannot say a greater truth in any words!

I am aware of the diverse expositions of this text. It deals with love and judgment, and identification with Christ. If he abides in us and we in him, we need not be afraid at the last great day. His perfect love in us casts out fear. One well-known writer was much puzzled as to the meaning of the verse, until he read it to mean, "As he is with regard to judgment.... He will never come into judgment and since he and I are identified, neither will I." The applications of it stretch out in all directions, but I am going to take the text just as it stands in its simplest form, and just as it appears to the ordinary reader. "As he is, so are we in this world."

Here are nine little words that fall apart into three sets of three words each. *"As he is—so are we—in this world."*

"As he is," not, mind you, "As he *was*." There are those who see only the Christ of Galilee centuries ago as our example, and vainly try lifting themselves by their own bootstraps to be like him. He is indeed our example, and if we are to walk as he walked we must know how he walked when he was among us. But he is infinitely more than an example out of the past. So much has happened since the days of his flesh. He died and rose and ascended and is glorified; he stands at the Father's right hand and in all his glory will return one day. As he *is,* so are we; not of course in degree, but in kind. If we trust him we are partakers of his nature, and

what is his, is ours. All that he is *today* we share. Our experience is limited by our faith, understanding, and capacity; but we are not pale copies of a model furnished nineteen centuries ago. As he *is*, so are we.

Then, "As he is, *so ARE we....*" Again, it does not say merely "so should we be." Indeed we ought, but that is not what it says. Nor do we read, "As he is, so may we be." Indeed we may and can be as he is, but that is not the text; nor does it say, "As he is, so shall we be." We shall indeed be like him one day, for we shall see him as he is; but that glorious prospect is not in mind here. "So *are* we" here and now. What he is up there, we are down here. If we have been born again, he lives in us. We are the projection of him into this day and age. In a Christian, Christ lives again. We are becoming saints but we also *are* saints. A Christian is a being and a becoming. We are far from perfection, but in so far as we let him fill and control our lives, "as he is, so are we in this world."

Finally, we are as he is *in this world;* not just in church where it is not too difficult to look pious on Sunday morning; not in some favored spot in holy seclusion "far from the madding crowd's ignoble strife—" *"in this world—"* this wicked, foul, polluted and perverted Sodom and Gomorrah; in the old rat race, the old salt mines, every day of the week. I wouldn't give a nickel for a Christianity that cannot be lived out in the kitchen, on a pagan college campus, on the job in a shop full of cursing sinners, or in an office where Jesus Christ is only a byword. This world is no friend of grace to help us on to God. Although Christians are not of it, they are *in* it, and it is a good training ground for soldiers of the cross. We are the light of the world, and light is needed in dark places. We are not saved to out-dazzle each other at church and in religious conventions. Our Savior said, "As thou hast sent me into the world, even so have I also sent them into the world" (John 17:18). "As he is, so are we *in this world.*"

This throws a lot of light on what a Christian really is. "So *are* we...." What we believe is important, but a man may believe correctly with his head without anything happening in his heart. What we do is important, but a man may do things a Christian ought to do and still be an unconverted Pharisee. Creed and conduct have their places, but we are dealing here with character; not what we believe and do but what we are. A Christian is not the sum total of what he believes in his head and does with his hands, but of what he is in his heart. He must be a partaker of the divine nature of Jesus Christ by the miracle of the new birth. Only then can he have boldness in the day of judgment. Christians are not just nice people; they are new creatures. Old things have passed away and all things have become new. If one is what he has always been, he is not a Christian, for a Christian is something new.

Nowadays we ask people to "accept Christ." That is not a New Testament term. We are told to believe on the Lord Jesus Christ, trust him with the heart (Acts 16:31) and receive him (John 1:12). "Accept" gives the impression that our Lord is standing hat-in-hand, awaiting our verdict on him. After all, he invites us to come to him; and what matters most is whether he accepts us. We hear about "taking Christ as Savior." The Scriptures do not tell us to take him *as* anything. We are to receive *him*, period. If that were better understood today there would be none of this idea that we can take Christ as Savior now, and maybe years later take him as Lord, as though these were two separate experiences—something not taught in the New Testament at all.

However, there is a sense, if properly understood, when we do take Christ as a wife takes a husband. In the New Testament, marriage is used to illustrate the relationship of Christ and the church (Ephesians 5:32). A Christian is married to Christ (Romans 7:4). Paul espoused the Corinthian Christians to one husband (2 Corinthians 11:2). When a woman marries a man she takes him for all that he is. She may not know all that he is and may discover more later that she did not know when she said, "I do"; but for better or worse she took him as he was, became identified with him, and they became one. In a very real sense, from then on as he is so is she in this world. His joys and sorrows are hers; his successes and failures are hers; his past, present, and future are hers. In this divorce-ridden generation, too many accept the privileges but not the responsibilities of marriage. By the same token, our church rolls are filled with members who accepted the privileges of church membership, but refuse to assume its obligations. They accepted the Saviorhood of Christ but not His Lordship. Some of them are what James called adulterers and adulteresses, untrue to their marriage vows to Jesus Christ, friends of the world and enemies of God.

When a believer receives Christ he takes him for all that he is, both Savior and Lord. All that Christ has becomes ours, and all that we have becomes his. It is about time we discovered the magnitude of this transaction in this day when people equate becoming a Christian with joining a church—pretty much as one joins a secret order or a civic club. This is a contract for time and eternity between a sinner and the Son of God. This is free salvation, but it is not cheap. It cost the Son of God his life to purchase it, and it costs us all we are and have when we receive it, for thenceforth we belong to Jesus Christ; we are not our own; we are bought with a price. We do not pay for our salvation, for "Jesus paid it all," as we sing sometimes, but "all to him we owe," as the next line declares. This is not bondage; it is the glorious liberty of the sons of God. We are one with him in the family of our Father; and we shall not fear in the day of judgment, for perfect love casts out fear. We bear the family resemblance, and "as he is, so are we in this world." Think what would happen in our churches if we ever woke up to this!

When we become Christians, Christ's life becomes our life. He did not come to earth to teach us a better way to live. He came that we might have *life*. Paul did not say, "To me, to live is to live like Christ or for Christ." He said, "To me to live *is* Christ" (Philippians 1:12). We cannot live the Christian life until we have the Christian life to live. Every Christian is an extension of Christ's life. Paul did not say, "I'm living for Christ." He said, "Christ liveth in me" (Gal. 2:20).

When we receive Christ, *his joys become our joys*. What makes him glad, makes us rejoice. How about that? What do you rejoice about? I am not speaking of mere happiness which depends on what happens. Do you rejoice in God's will in your life and in the lives of others? His joys are ours because his joy is our joy. He said, "These things have I spoken unto you, that my joy might remain in you, and that your joy might be full" (John 15:11). When we see the things most church members enjoy today, we wonder whether they have ever known anything about his joy!

Furthermore, *his sorrows become our sorrows.* We can grieve the Holy Spirit. Our Lord wept over Jerusalem, and he is burdened over a lukewarm church and a lost world. Any Christian who can take it easy and not be saddened over the state of the church and the world today is out of fellowship with his Lord. The Savior even got angry on occasion, and we need to share his indignation at the devil and all the works of the devil, instead of boasting broad-mindedness about the things that God condemns. We smile today at what breaks the heart of the Savior in this generation that makes comedy out of tragedy.

When we are joined to Christ, *his friends become our friends.* He said, "Ye are my friends, if ye do whatsoever I command you" (John 15:14). A friend of Jesus is one who obeys him. That leaves a lot of church members out in the cold! Christians should be friendly to everybody, but there is a higher friendship known only to those who love our Lord. What we call fellowship when we gossip over our coffee at some church suppers is often just sociability under religious auspices, and not necessarily the communion of saints. "We know that we have passed from death unto life because we love the brethren" (1 John 3:14), and we love the brethren because our Lord's friends are our friends and "as he is, so are we in this world."

From this it follows that when we take Christ, *his enemies are our enemies.* Paul writes of "enemies of the cross of Christ" (Philippians 3:18). James says that the friend of the world is the enemy of God. Christians have no business hobnobbing with men who deny the blood of Christ or church worldlings, whom James calls adulterers, because they are untrue to their Christian vows. A wife who is eighty-five percent faithful to her husband is not faithful at all. There is no such thing as part-time loyalty to Jesus Christ. It is all or nothing. The man who plays with the enemies of Christ is a traitor to his Lord. We cannot be popular with a world that crucified our Lord, for "as the Master, so shall the servant be," and "as he is, so are we in this world."

When we are united to Christ, *his cross becomes our cross.* This cross is not ordinary trouble, for everybody has trouble. It is not chastisement, for that is not voluntary. The cross of Christ we choose ourselves. "If any man will come after me, let him deny himself, and take up his cross, and follow me" (Matthew 16:24). His cross is the trouble, the persecution, the reproach we suffer because of our identification with him—because we are Christians. It is what we sing about:

> To the old rugged cross I will ever be true,
> It's shame and reproach gladly bear.

This kind of cross-bearing Christian is not popular with this world and never will be. Simeon said that our Lord would be "spoken against," and the Jews in Rome told Paul that everywhere his religion was "spoken against." I am not thinking now of run-of-the-mill church members. It is fashionable to be a church member these days. It is a status symbol. It helps business and looks good in an obituary. A great world church is shaping up before our eyes in these last days, having a form of godliness but denying the power thereof. It will be stylish to belong to this church, but the despised sect of the Nazarenes—the followers of the Way, true New Testament Christians—will be called the scum of the earth and will be a spectacle to the world for the scandal of the cross.

There is one thing more. When we become Christ's and he becomes ours, *his future is our future!* And what a future! "If we suffer, we shall also reign with him" (2 Timothy 2:12). He is coming back; the meek shall inherit the earth, and the saints shall judge the world. We may not look like it now, but our day is coming. All kinds of groups are trying to take over this old world. They are marching and demonstrating and shouting and waving their banners around the earth. The newsreels are loaded with them, but you never see the real future rulers, for we do not demonstrate that way. We are not organized on that pattern. There are no statistics available. You will find some of us in all the churches. We are waiting for our King to return; and when he does, everybody will know who we are and how many, for we will come into our own. The kingdoms of this world will become the kingdoms of our Lord and his Christ, who shall reign until all his enemies are put under his feet, and where'er the sun doth his successive journeys run.

Are you married to this heavenly Bridegroom? We are accustomed to brides walking down aisles to church altars to say, "I take this man...." I invite you to a far greater altar to say, "I take Jesus Christ to be my Savior and Lord. All I am and have is henceforth his, not 'until death do us part,' as we say in the wedding ceremony, for death will not part us. This is for time and eternity." Some have never received him. Others have received him but have been unfaithful and need to renew their vows, saying:

> O Jesus, I have promised
> To serve thee to the end;
> Be thou forever near me,
> My Master and my friend:
> I shall not fear the battle
> If thou art by my side,
> Nor wander from the pathway
> If thou wilt be my guide.

Marked Men

ONE of the attractions of the New York World's Fair was the General Motors Futurama, depicting the wonder world of the future to be created by American technological know-how. Long ago an old preacher sat on a lonely rock in a restless sea, and saw "the things which shall be hereafter" (Revelation 1:19), God's "Futurama." In this vision he saw a fearful beast rise out of the earth who would eventually cause all, "both small and great, rich and poor, free and bond, to receive a mark in their right hand, or in their foreheads: And that no man might buy or sell, save he that had the mark, or the name of the beast, or the number of his name" (Revelation 13:16, 17).

Whatever this means, it will be the ultimate in regimentation. We are well on our way to that sad hour. We are being primed for that day. Already we are numbered, tagged, and labeled from A to Z, from auto license to zip code. The average American is a social security number with a wallet full of credit cards. We are being processed and brainwashed far in advance, and made ready for the mark of the beast. Of course all the marks we now wear are but tokens, foreshadowings, or straws in the wind; but they do point up the trend. (In the early days of Franklin D. Roosevelt's New Deal, some thought the N.R.A. was the mark of the beast!)

Already the human race is being standardized and homogenized into facelessness. The mountains are being leveled into one plain. Individuality is being steamrollered into uniformity until we will be as alike as a row of telephone poles or eggs in a crate. This is true not only under communism, but everywhere. It is not necessary to be communistic to be evil. One is reminded of the unholy mixture of the sons of God with the daughters of men before the flood—the mixing of iron and clay in Daniel's image. Black and white are being merged into grey. Social reformers are cooking up mulligan stews and trying to improve the bad eggs of society by scrambling them into one omelet.

Young people talk about being different. Never was a generation of youngsters more alike. They dress alike, talk alike, act alike. Consider the dictatorship of fashion today. Plenty of women wear garb in which they would not be caught dead if it were not the style. I read recently that the sameness of television personalities is due to the fact that they must not outshine the commercials! In England, a workman was dropped from his labor organization because he did his work too well. His excellence showed up the shoddy performance of his fellow workers. Even in the ministry, where more and more preachers are turned out by assembly line methods, a colorful minister with original message and method is frowned upon as an unwholesome departure from the pattern. Student uprisings on university campuses are traced in part to what is called "creeping impersonality." "Nobody knows our names," they complain.

The nations are being mingled into one world state. The churches are being amalgamated into one world church. Many good people are deceived thereby and many well-meaning souls endorse it, but it will be the harlot that rides the beast in that same Patmos Futurama. Togetherness is the order of the day. Liberal and conservative Christianity blend, as doctrinal lines are erased and unbelief is equated with truth, in the public eye, by peaceful coexistence in one vast ecumenical super church. There is a true ecumenicity, of course: the unity of the Spirit; but this is not that. The world and the church are married today, and what is thought to be the world becoming more Christian is only Christians becoming more worldly. The sacred and profane are mingled as the world shouts, "Hallelujah," and hymns give way to hootenannies.

It is gloriously true of the children of God by faith in Christ Jesus that "There is neither Jew nor Greek...bond nor free...male nor female: for ye are all one in Christ Jesus" (Galatians 3:28). No intelligent Christian will confuse this with the false brotherhood of man now being superimposed on an unregenerate humanity.

Even Nikita Khrushchev (who may have been deposed because he was becoming too colorful an individual and was therefore supplanted by nonentities) said during his American tour, "We want to build a land where there is no enmity, where there is complete equality such as was preached by Christ." Dr. H. A. Ironside said of the rider on the white horse in the Patmos Futurama, "Man's last effort to bring in a reign of order and peace while Christ is still rejected, the devil's cunning scheme for bringing a mock millennium without Christ." Dr. Torrance of Edinburgh, at opposite poles from Dr. Ironside on much of his eschatology said, nevertheless, "Six hundred and sixty-six is the number of so-called Christian civilization without Jesus Christ. It is the number of every attempt to organize the world in a form that appears marvelously Christian but is in reality anti-Christian." No Bible believer will be deceived by any of these false Utopias now preached by old Adam, even when he wears his Sunday clothes and quotes Scripture. Such a Christian knows the difference between Babylon from below and the New Jerusalem from above. He is not interested so much in the Great Society (which ex-president Eisenhower called "Instant Paradise") but rather in the Good Society—the heavenly commonwealth of the sons of God. He will not be swept off his feet by those who try to make moral issues of political projects. Like Micaiah, he will not be pressured into making it unanimous by four hundred rubber stamp, false prophets bidding Ahab and Jehoshaphat go up against Ramoth Gilead.

In this era of the organization man, this "creeping impersonality—" this facelessness—is making it more and more difficult to be somebody in a day of zeros. Of course God's people will have been removed before Antichrist finally rules over a streamlined humanity, but even now, in the blueprint stages, we feel the increasing pressures of conformity. Anyone who refuses to be stampeded before the avalanche, and anyone who refuses to listen to the siren voice of the mock angel (Satan disguised as a seraph) is called unchristian, unloving, a square, a reactionary, or a hindrance in the path of progress. If he shows the least sign of original thought, or of daring to stand alone for an unpopular cause, he is a marked man. Even in the religious world this is true; and what will it be like in the day when only one church, the world church, is recognized and legalized by the state? I repeat my comment on the magazine article describing the church of tomorrow: "Thank God, I won't be here to see it!" Let it not be forgotten that when the Man of Sin appears, he will be at first most gracious and charming. He would deceive if possible the very elect. So attractive will be his presence, and so appealing his program, that to oppose him will seem downright absurdity. Today, even in the advance and preliminary stages this is true, and even to suspect the false prophets and pseudo-Christs now on the horizon is regarded as gross stupidity. The man who refuses to keep step with the procession now forming will be the target of the powers of darkness, "spiritual agents from the very headquarters of evil" (Ephesians 6:12, Phillips). He will be beset by strange maladies in body, mind, and spirit, ostracized by his brainwashed contemporaries who ride the wave of the future. As the lawlessness and demonism now already rampant head toward the climax, all who love the mystery of godliness will feel the venomous hatred of all who aid and abet the mystery of iniquity. Because of the abounding anarchy the love of most will wax cold as our Savior said, and the faithful few will feel as alone as John on Patmos. As citizens of the New Jerusalem they are strangers in Babylon, aliens and exiles looking for the city that is soon coming down.

The brand of the beast is not yet with us, because he himself has not yet appeared; but preliminary markings are already in order, and men are being readied for the final branding by wearing little badges now in vogue. None of them is the mark of the beast, but they get us used to being cataloged in a faceless aggregation; and it will not seem too strange when we reach the ultimate.

Society is being collectivized into a faceless mass and the big word is "conformity." We are not to be conformed to this world nor let it squeeze us into its mold (Romans 12:2), but the way out is not by mere nonconformity. "... be ye transformed by the renewing of your mind..." (Romans 12:2). We are not to live by merely saying "no" to the world, but by saying "yes" to God. We were predestinated to be conformed to the image of God's Son. We can major in not conforming to this world and fail to be conformed to our Lord. If Satan cannot make world conformists of us, he will make us so busy with nonconformity that we become only Pharisees, separated from sinners but not from sin.

There are other marked men besides those who bear the brand of the beast. Thomas looked for the prints of the nails and the spear in the risen Lord, and an unbelieving world looks today for the marks of the cross in us Christians. Thomas knew that his Lord had died. What he wanted to know was: is he alive? The best evidence of a living Christ is a Christ-like Christian. Paul bore in his body the marks of the Lord Jesus, and we ought to manifest our identification with the Savior in his death and resurrection. Alas, we wear medals but not many scars!

> Hast thou no scar?
> No hidden scar on foot or side or hand?
> I hear thee sung as mighty in the land;
> I hear them hail thy bright ascendant star.
> Hast thou no scar?
> No wound, no scar?
> Yet as the Master shall the servant be;
> And pierced are the feet that follow me;
> But thine are whole; can he have followed far
> Who has no wound, no scar?

Paul spoke of himself as "Always bearing about in the body the dying of the Lord Jesus, that the life also of Jesus might be made manifest in our body" (2 Corinthians 4:10). He wore no medals but he had scars aplenty. The only stocks and bonds he knew were stocks for his feet and bonds for his wrists! He was a marked man. The marks of the Lord Jesus were his credentials! What pulpit committee these days thinks of that? Education, appearance, abilities, degrees, and medals, yes, but who asks, "Does he bear evidence of being God's man?" Paul wore the stigmata, the branding marks of a slave—not a paid servant, but a bondslave of Jesus Christ.

We always bear the brand of our master. This cocktail and cigarette generation advertises itself with dissipated face, trembling hands, and jittery behavior. All the sedatives cannot quiet, nor cosmetics hide, their scars. One need not be a psychiatrist to read the signs of vicious temper, hidden hatred, and evil thoughts.

> The false, the deceit, that you bear in your heart
> Will not stay inside when it first gets a start;
> For sinew and blood are a thin veil of lace;
> What you wear in your heart you wear on your face.

On the other hand, prayer and the Word and godly living show up in our faces too. Moses wist not that his face shone. The best saints are least conscious of it, but they bear in their countenances the marks of the Master. That is well, for

> The only heaven some will ever see
> Is the heaven they see in you and me.

Years of holy living make a difference! Abraham Lincoln said a man couldn't help how he looked when he was born, but he could help how he looked after forty years. God's men are branded; they are men of the cross, bringing the message of the cross, bearing the marks of the cross.

It has been said many times that a cross is an "I" crossed out. The cross means death to sin, to self, to the world. That does not come easily in its daily realization. The old nature rebels against it. Peter confessed the Christ but with almost the next breath he denied the cross. Paul said, "I *am crucified* with Christ" (Galatians 2:20). For the Christian it is already a fact; we make it real in experience as we "reckon," "yield," and "obey" (Romans 6).

Marked Men

Long ago I heard a missionary tell about an African native Christian. He still had a bad temper that got him into trouble. He heard one day that we are crucified with Christ. To make it more real he burned, with a hot iron, the mark of a cross in the palm of his right hand. He explained later, "When I get angry and clench my fist, I feel the scar of that cross and it reminds me that I am crucified with Christ." A crude way to do it indeed, but it would be well if we could remind ourselves as effectively that we are marked men!

We are marked men because we follow a *marked man.* "He was wounded for our transgressions, he was bruised for our iniquities: the chastisement of our peace was upon him; and with his stripes we are healed" (Isaiah 53:5). When Thomas saw those wounds, he cried, "My Lord and my God" (John 20:28). "Blessed are they that have not seen, and yet have believed" (John 20:29). One of these days we shall all see him. We read that his Name shall be in our foreheads (Revelation 22:4). That is the opposite of the mark of the beast; it is the autograph of our Lord. Would that all autograph seekers made sure of that one! When we see him we shall know him. "When redeemed by his side we shall stand" for we shall know him "by the prints of the nails in his hand."

Salt of the Earth

Ye are the salt of the earth: but if the salt have lost his savour, wherewith shall it be salted? it is thenceforth good for nothing, but to be cast out, and to be trodden under foot of men (Matthew 5:13).

IT might have seemed ridiculous to a casual bystander for Jesus to say to a handful of ordinary men, "You are the salt of the earth, and I am sending you out to permeate and infiltrate and season the whole world." Yet that little band, that pinch of salt, started something that has survived the centuries and changed the history of mankind.

Our Lord used the simplest figures of speech. Nothing is plainer, more universal, and old-fashioned than salt. It is such a common commodity that we take it for granted; but if suddenly no salt could be had, what a difference that would make! What would life be without salt! A little boy said, "Salt is what tastes bad when you don't have it." Christians are the salt of the earth and we ought to make a difference!

Not all church members are salt of the earth – only bornagain Christians who share the life of Christ and are partakers of his nature. When our Lord spoke of salt losing its savor, he did not mean that salt can ever cease to be salt. Sodium chloride does not deteriorate. One must think of mountains of salt as at the Dead Sea, mixed with other deposits. The hot sun evaporates the sea water and leaves the salt crystals. Today the professing church, this gigantic institutionalism with so much of the world in it, and so many unsaved church members in it—with so little true salt—has no "taste," makes no difference and is *good for nothing*, as our Lord said, but to be cast out and trodden underfoot. That is the state of so-called Christendom: the mountain of salt has no savor. It needs to be processed to separate the true salt from all other elements. It may take the burning sun of persecution to evaporate the false and leave the true. One thing is certain: the salt is not making much difference in this world today, mixed with a mountain of worldliness, false doctrine, and imitation Christianity.

When our Lord said, "Ye are the salt of the earth," he implied that the earth is corrupt and that society is rotten. We do not salt living things to preserve them. Humanity is a decaying carcass awaiting the vultures of judgment. Society today, for all our culture, scientific know-how, and boasted civilization, is in a state of decomposition. Only the presence of God's people, the salt of the earth, keeps it from spoiling overnight. When the church is removed, the putrefaction will be complete. America itself is a decaying nation. Our national symbol is the eagle, but if the present rate of moral deterioration continues, it ought to be a vulture!

Now if we Christians are the salt of the earth, we ought to remember that the only way salt can do any good is by being brought into direct contact with whatever it is meant to affect. We call it "involvement" nowadays. We are not to withdraw from the world like the old mystics. Garden seeds never become vegetables by remaining in their pretty packages. They must be emptied into the dirty old ground, die, and come up again. "Except a corn of wheat fall into the ground and die, it abideth alone: but if it die, it bringeth forth much fruit" (John 12:24). We Christians can become so clannish that we lose contact with the very world we were meant to influence. Nowadays we have our own schools, recreation, hotels, and insurance companies. All this is good, but we can run clear off the reservation and forget that we are the light of the world and a light is needed in a dark place. Instead of the salt permeating the world around us, we can be content to sit in our saltcellars on Sunday morning, far removed from a needy and decaying humanity, and so dainty and fastidious that we wouldn't touch a dying world with a forty foot pole. We are willing to be missionaries after the world has been disinfected!

But we are the salt to disinfect it! Jesus mixed with publicans and sinners. We are not going to have much effect on this evil world sitting in religious meetings all dressed up unless we go out to minister. Salt in a saltshaker is of no earthly use. Only when it gets out of the shaker is it effective! None of us likes to be rubbed into a decaying society. It goes against the grain. Only the love of Christ and a love for souls can overcome our natural distaste for unpleasant situations.

On the other hand, too many Christians are not only in the world but of it—so mixed with it that, instead of their salting the world, the world is spoiling them. It is always one or the other. To change the figure, we are, as Alexander McLaren says, either hammer or anvil. If we are not warming the world, the world is cooling us. We lose our savor; we become insipid, tasteless Christians. There is nothing to smack the lips over. We are "good for nothing." What are *you* good for?

Salt has a *seasoning* influence. There ought to be a flavor, a tang, a relish, and a zest about us Christians. Someone has said that our main trouble today is not that our doctrine is false, but that our experience is flat.

> In vain we tune our formal songs;
> In vain we strive to rise;
> Hosannas languish on our tongues,
> And our devotion dies.

It is the flatness of salt without savor.

Salt *preserves.* Civilization has been saved from destruction by the restraining influence of the Holy Spirit in Christians. Salt prevents decay and restrains corruption. One godly person in a group will restrain evil conversation. In his eyes, a vile person is condemned. God's pinch of salt in the earth has preserved it from total decay.

Salt *purifies* and *cleanses.* The best gargle for a sore throat is plain salt water. The church of Jesus Christ has had a purifying influence wherever it has gone. You may think that your community is in a bad state, but take out the church and you would not want to live there. Yet many live as though there were no church there! For all its faults and failures, God's pinch of salt keeps the community from being a cesspool of iniquity completely.

Salt *heals*. Lives are changed, souls saved, homes rescued from disaster, broken hearts mended, sorrows eased, burdens lifted, sick bodies and minds made well because of the antiseptic and therapeutic power of the Holy Spirit working through God's people, the salt of the earth. Think of the arguments that have been settled, the quarrels, conflicts, and divisions straightened out by the peacemaking power of the gospel. The world is inflamed and sore with hatred today, and the only balm that can heal these wounds is not legislation and reformation, but the healing power of love in the hearts of Christians.

Salt *creates thirst*. God's people should develop in the hearts of men a desire to know God. We ought so to live that others would want the peace and joy they see in us. Does anybody want to be a Christian like *you*? The best argument for Christianity is a Christian.

How are we, as the salt of the earth, going to bring this seasoning, preserving, purifying, healing, and thirst-producing power to bear on our homes, our neighbors, our communities, and our society? Salt does its work quietly. There is no noise about it. One does not have to wear a badge proclaiming "I am a Christian." The Pharisees paraded their religion and our Lord called them hypocrites and play-actors. Of course, there is a time and place for public testimony. Too many are like Arctic rivers: frozen at the mouth. It is a day of good tidings and we hold our peace. Ours is an articulate faith. It talks, it confesses Jesus as Lord with the mouth; but if the salt of the earth is to have much effect on pagan society, little bands of dedicated Christians must permeate every area of life with the witness of the gospel. The light of the world must shine where the darkness is. The sick need the physician, not the well.

We are like a room-full of lamps, all brilliantly lighted and trying to out-dazzle each other on Sunday. We enjoy our own company so much that we become members of an exclusive club instead of missionaries. The early church at Jerusalem had to be shaken out of its saltcellar by persecution, and scattered everywhere preaching the Word. We need Christian students in high school and college, as a cell of disciples making Christ known by life and lip to their schoolmates. We need Christian business men infiltrating their business circles and civic clubs, witnessing to their associates. We need Christian women in suburbia, quietly letting their lights shine up and down the blocks, not just in the missionary meeting at church. We need Christians in politics, and as mechanics, truck drivers, dentists, nurses, doctors, teachers, capable of seasoning, cleansing, healing, preserving, creating thirst, permeating, and infiltrating. This is our business. Too many church members have the idea that to go to church on Sunday, give some money in a duplex envelope, and maybe do a little "church work," is the full extent of their responsibility. Actually, we go to church to learn how to live better for Jesus Christ, as the salt of the earth, all the rest of the week. Pastors, teachers, and evangelists are for the perfecting of the saints for the work of *their* ministry. Every Christian is a minister and his ministry is to be the salt of the earth, to penetrate, infiltrate and permeate society for Jesus Christ. If he is not doing that, he is salt without savor and good for nothing.

We are not going to convert the world. It will not be Christianized but it can be evangelized. We ought to Christianize as much of it as we can, win all the converts we can, make all the impact we can, capture as much of this civilization as we can, put all the good men in office we can, and season and purify and heal all we can. It will not be easy. Salt has another characteristic I have not mentioned: salt *irritates*. When the salt of God's truth is rubbed into this diseased old world, sick souls may smart. When the light is turned on, some will wince. The devil hates the gospel and fights back. Billy Sunday used to say, "They tell me I rub the fur the wrong way. I don't; let the cat turn around!" We are not the sugar of the earth—nor the vinegar—but we are salt and we will not be welcomed by a generation full of wounds, bruises and putrefying sores. (Today there is a new non-irritating brand of Christianity, but it is without offense and without effect.)

We need to get into the salt business and we must start with a few. This is God's program today. It sounds old-fashioned, but salt is old-fashioned, sin is old-fashioned, and so is the gospel. We have been tickling palates with fancy flavors, spicy relishes, and clever recipes borrowed from the world. Too many pulpit gourmets and theological epicures with menus from Hollywood are trying to please the jaded appetites of a fed up humanity. We need old-fashioned salt, and if we do not start producing more of it in our churches, we shall be good for nothing but to be cast out and trodden under foot of men.

Knowing What To Do

And of the children of Issachar, which were men that had understanding of the times, to know what Israel ought to do... (1 Chronicles 12:32).

And that, knowing the time, that now it is high time to awake out of sleep: for now is our salvation nearer than when we believed (Romans 13:11).

THE children of Issachar had more than a knowledge of the times: they had an understanding of the times that produced a knowledge of what God's people ought to do. Modern experts have a knowledge of the times. Listen to the news reporters; read the columnists; hear Dr. Toynbee for instance. But they do not understand the times. When men do not know the Scriptures and the power of God, they err, our Lord said. Certainly these men do not know what God's people ought to do today. The most important business we have is to find out which way God is going and get going in that direction. If we are to chart our course correctly, it must be done in the light of several tremendous truths.

First, there is *the promise of our Lord's return.* The church missed the road centuries ago when it stopped looking for the King to come back and began building the kingdom down here. There is indeed a spiritual kingdom, which is not meat and drink but righteousness, peace, and joy in the Holy Spirit, and the reign of God in the hearts of men. The visible kingdom will not be brought in by education, legislation, and reformation, even under religious auspices. It will be set up when the King comes back. If that were understood, misguided souls would not be riding all kinds of queer band-wagons, trying to bring in a counterfeit millennium, and superimposing a false kingdom of heaven—a profane paradise—on an unregenerate society.

The early church went forth with the proclamation of Christ come, living in the prospect of Christ coming by the power of Christ contemporary: "Lo, I am with you" (Matthew 28:20). I believe that we are in the last days. We have had many of the signs of the times before, but not concurrent as in the present pattern.

However, we have more to do than to sit with folded hands, waiting to be rescued by Christ's return. There is a second consideration: *the possibility of a great revival*—a visitation from above, with God coming down in a latter rain of a great awakening. There have been such mighty occurrences in the past when there were nationwide movings of great multitudes, like a wheat field before a summer wind. We have not seen that in this generation, and it is doubtful whether there can be a deep revival among such shallow people. Revival, however, does not have all the answers. Someone has compared such resurgences to a sale in a department store. The sale may be more spectacular, but the main business is done in the daily merchandising the year round. Pentecost was a great day, but the steady growth came as the Lord added to the church daily. Revivals make headlines, but when the books are added up at the last day, it will be found that the main work was done by the faithful preaching of ordinary pastors, the daily witnessing of ordinary Christians, and soul-winning in home and church. We do need revival and while we cannot produce it, we can pray and prepare for it.

If the Lord tarries and revival does not come, there is the *prospect of retribution*—the judgment of God on unrepentant men. America is a Belshazzar's feast, and that feast was marked by *revelry, Revelation* and *retribution*. America is on a national binge, being not yet two hundred years old and dying of moral cancer before our eyes. The decaying carcass awaits the vultures. God has written his warning on the wall and there are few Daniels who will dare to read it. Daniel did not say that he couldn't read it. There are ministers today who cannot read

God's handwriting. They do not understand the times nor the meaning of history. Daniel did not read something else. There are false prophets who interpret Revelation to mean what God never meant. The book of Revelation tells us of a final Babylon, ecclesiastical and political: the final amalgamation of collectivized humanity into a world church and world state under Antichrist. We need a Daniel who can stand in the midst of this Babylon, turn down the rich fare of Nebuchadnezzar, defy the decrees of Darius, and in the midst of the revelry read the Revelation on the wall, predicting retribution to a trembling Belshazzar. The *Interpreter's Bible* to the contrary and notwithstanding, Daniel understood the times and knew what God's people ought to do.

Now, while we await the *return* and pray for *revival* and face *retribution,* is there anything more that Christians can do than just be faithful? Is it the best that we can do just to maintain business as usual? Sometimes we hear church services announced "as usual." Maybe that is what is wrong with them! Nothing else is as usual these days. We need to go on an emergency basis, for the hour is too late and the need too great to go about it as though we had a thousand years in which to complete the job. We have no business living ordinary lives in such extraordinary times.

Against the background of *the promise of our Lord's return, the possibility of revival,* and *the prospect of retribution,* we need to project a *program of the remnant.* By that I mean we ought to gather a Master's minority, the faithful few, the company of the committed, a spearhead of expendables, the church within the church. Our Lord stands at the door of Laodicea in these last days and says, "If any man (anyone) hear my voice and open the door, I will come in" (Revelation 3:20). He is calling out the assembly of the anyones!

Dr. Torrey used to say: "In order to have a revival, let a few members of any church get thoroughly right with God." We have been doing things the extensive way in our church life. It is time to start doing things the intensive way. We've been doing it the big way; it is time to start doing it the little way. You will remember that God told Gideon he had too many soldiers in his original army of thirty-two thousand. He had too many of the kind he had for the kind of battle he was out to fight. The church is in spiritual warfare, and the weapons of that warfare are not carnal. The average run-of-the-mill church member is untrained and unqualified for this kind of fighting. We have too many of the kind that most of them are, and if we won the battle, we would take the credit for it ourselves, as God told Gideon. We are not going to win this war by a motley mob of the cowards and careless, but by a minority committed in holy desperation—a dedicated few to permeate and infiltrate the world as the salt of the earth.

The faithful minority in our churches cannot get at the unreached multitude outside because of the unfaithful majority on the inside. We cannot reach the goal for stumbling over our own team. We furnish our own interference. We need to rally a Gideon's Band, a bundle of human kindling wood who will instead of letting the majority inside the church and the multitude outside chill their zeal, warm up the church and start a fire in the world as our Lord came to do. This is the strategy of the remnant and the only program that will work today. If it be objected that such procedure would mean two churches in every church, do we not have that situation already: those who are active for Christ and those who by their very inactivity for him are active against him? Did he not say, "he that gathereth not with me scattereth abroad" (Matthew 12:30)?

So, while we wait for the return of our Lord and pray for revival and face retribution, let us rally a remnant with understanding of the times to know what God's people ought to do.

The pastor should lead the way in recruiting the church within the church. There will be problems. Sometimes church policy is in the hands of men and women who know nothing of New Testament standards and couldn't care less. The pastor must decide whether to bring the flag back to the regiment or try to make the regiment catch up with the flag. The temptation will be strong to accept the status quo and be an ordinary church. Of course, no church is perfect. The New Testament churches were not perfect, but they had a standard and dealt with anyone who tried to lower that standard. Paul did not accept conditions in Corinth as normal. They were subnormal and he would have them normal. We have been content with the subnormal for so long, however, that normal New Testament Christianity appears to most church members to be abnormal!

Of course it goes without saying that this remnant, this church within the church, must not become a little clique of super saints proud of their spiritual superiority. Sometimes these super saints become snooper saints, spying on all who do not dot their "i's" and cross their "t's" to suit them. A nucleus of born-again, Spirit-filled, Bible-believing, Christ-centered, soul-winning disciples is the only answer today. Only these will have understanding of the times and know what to do.

Let the Church Be the Church!

SOME time ago, in a church convention, I listened to a speaker doing his best to stir up the saints about the program for next year. The platform was filled with charts, placards, and diagrams listing goals galore: so many converts to be baptized, so many dollars to be raised. Although the speaker tried hard to fan the flickering flame of enthusiasm, the people were tired; some left and the evening wore to a dull finish. I said to myself, "Something is wrong somewhere. I'm for baptizing this many converts and raising this much money, but if instead of our trying to arouse these jaded church members from without, they could have a revival within and become Spirit-filled flaming witnesses, we would win more converts and raise more money than all these placards call for."

I have listened to church leaders deplore the spiritual slump, and the drop in finances, baptisms, ministerial enrollment, and missionary volunteers. I have heard pastors bemoan the Friday night ball game, the inroads of television, the Sunday night worship at the altar of television. It seems to me that the wrong crowd is doing the worrying. In the early church, it was the enemies of the Lord and the powers of darkness who were agitated, wondering whereunto all this would grow. It was the devil's crowd who sat up late at night, devising countermeasures to stem the revolution that was sweeping the world. These gospel "world upsetters" had Satan on the defensive. The early Roman Christians were not afraid prayer meeting attendance would drop because there was a gladiatorial contest at the Colosseum. Nobody suggested a religious hootenanny to offset the appeal of the pagan bacchanalia. Buttons and bananas and "pack-the-pew" had not yet been employed to lure half-hearted church members to the house of God. The church was its own publicity; it brought consternation to entrenched evil and alarm to the strongholds of sin. If we had what they had, the other crowd would do the worrying.

Why should the church take a back seat every time a sideshow blows into town? We were here first! If we do not have enough vitality today to compete successfully with the world, the flesh, and the devil, maybe it doesn't matter much whether we have meetings or not. Certainly the answer does not lie in stubbornly holding on to the form when the power has departed, and waving the scabbard after the sword is gone. It does no good to wring our hands over the counter attractions of the age that steal our congregations. The greater tragedy is not that men love other things so much but that they love Christ so little. If the gospel can be sidetracked for such trivialities, it wouldn't mean much if we did meet at church to go through the hollow motions of a dead Christianity. I do not intend to grow ulcers worrying about ball games and television, but what does cause me many a serious thought is that our Christianity is so puny that these things make any difference. If we believed that God broke into history nineteen hundred years ago; that there walked in Galilee a man who was also God; that he died for our sins and arose bodily from the grave and is coming back to set up an everlasting kingdom; that he is the answer to every human need from the smallest to the greatest—if we believed all that and lived in the power of it, we wouldn't know these "vain things that charm us most" were in town! As it is now, that crowd hardly knows *we* are in town!

If the gospel cost God his Son, if it cost the Son his life, and if it holds the destiny of every soul on earth for heaven or hell, for time and eternity, then it cannot be a matter of ordinary significance. If it is what we claim for it—if it is an experience and not just a performance—then it cannot be merely one of our interests like the club and the lodge and golf and antiques and ceramics and stamp collecting. It grieves me that we have this treasure in earthen vessels, and that there is committed to our trust the key to every secret in the universe; yet it means so little to most of us that we give it the leftovers of our time and attention. We ought to be honest enough to give it priority, or take down our sign! It ought to make us hang our heads in shame that we do not get as excited over it as we do about a political election. If we do not really believe it, then we are hypocrites to preach and promote something which most of its adherents wouldn't miss if they lost it! There is something frightfully wrong when we have to beg most of them to come to church to hear it and few ever go from church to tell it. I never see most of the members of any church during a revival. Evidently they do not think revivals are worth attending. If I were an unbeliever and dropped into the average church during a so-called revival and saw a fraction of the membership trying to get more recruits to join the army of the Lord when most of the outfit had already gone AWOL, I would surmise that Christianity is not what it is supposed to be or that we have been sold a watered-down, cheap and easy brand; that we have been inoculated with such a mild form that we are immunized against the real thing. My concern is not that most of our people are such worldlings that the cause of Christ does not attract them; it is rather that they are such weak Christians that anything else attracts them! We Americans have become used to the gospel. Familiarity has bred complacency, if not contempt. We have grown up with it like the Nazarenes with Jesus and have heard it from childhood. We celebrate the incarnation at Christmas and the resurrection at Easter, but it is more like a fairy tale and nothing to get excited about. We don't mind contributing something to perpetuate it, but few of us would dream of going all out to practice it. Belonging to a church doesn't mean much. Almost anyone can get in, and nobody ever gets out. A traveler in South Africa once found some boys playing marbles with diamonds! What is precious to most of us was commonplace with them. So do we play church—sing songs, and recite phrases that ought to set the world on fire. What once made our forefathers shout in the aisles puts us to sleep in the pews.

I return to the illustration with which I began. If Christians would just be Christians, if the church would just be the church, our brother at the convention with all his diagrams, charts, and goals would see greater results than his placards call for. More converts, more money, more missionaries, increased church attendance—all of this would follow, and outside attractions would lose their charm. Church workers would not have to almost bribe church members in trying to persuade them to do what ought to come naturally because they love the Lord.

No preacher is more foolish than the one who lambasts his people for going to other places on prayer meeting night. They will go then for certain just to show their independence! Besides, if they sit miserably at church with their hearts somewhere else, perhaps they might as well be somewhere else! It has been said that Christianity began as a company of lay witnesses, but it has become a professional pulpitism financed by lay spectators. Sitting politely at a Sunday performance is a long way from starting out every morning to be a flaming missionary for Jesus Christ in the shop, at the office, at school, at work, or at play, every day in the week. Lenin once said something to the effect that he would rather have a hundred fanatics than a thousand placid followers. We Christians are placid enough these days, and most of us are so far below standard that a normal Christian would be considered a fanatic.

We have been entrusted with the greatest mission and message on earth, but we have become used to it and now, for the most part, we go through the outward motions without the inner motive. We are actors in a religious play at church, but when we walk out of the doors, we are ourselves again. Jesus called that hypocrisy. This whole business will never come alive again except through repentance, confession of sin, getting right with God and men, giving up the world, submitting to the lordship of Christ, and being filled with the Spirit. That is a price most church members are not willing to pay, but until they are, we shall continue to sweat it out—raising budgets and reaching goals by our own wits, chopping with the axe handle when the axe head is gone.

The Bitter-Sweet Book

THE apostle John saw, in a vision, an angel standing with one foot on the earth and one on the sea, declaring that time should be delayed no longer. This is between the sixth and seventh trumpets of the Apocalypse and there is only one more trumpet to sound. Judgment is about to break in its final fury and the Antichrist will soon appear. The angel holds in his hand a scroll. It was a closed book in the fifth chapter, sealed with seven seals, and it contained the secret of destiny, the meaning of history, God's title deed to this earth, and his program for this age. Now it is an open book for the seals have been broken. John was told to eat the scroll. When he did, it was sweet when he tasted it but bitter when he swallowed it.

I am thinking of another book. The Bible is a "bitter-sweet" book. *It is sweet to the believer, bitter to the unbeliever.* It is a message of salvation for all who receive it, and a message of condemnation for all who reject it. Its message is a savor of life unto life and of death unto death. The same sun that shines on ice and melts it shines on clay and hardens it. The Bible humbles or hardens the human heart. "He that believeth on him is not condemned: but he that believeth not is condemned already" (John 3:18). If we hear it and do not do what it says, we deceive ourselves. It is not like Homer or Shakespeare. We do not go away the same after we have heard the Word of God. We have to do something about its message, for we cannot leave it alone. We may think we have done nothing about it, but it will do something to us.

Today, as in Isaiah's time, we are asked to prophesy smooth things and deceits; but we must preach both the wrath and love of God, for his Word is a bitter-sweet book. You had better be careful about that Bible lying around in your house, dusty and unread. More Bibles are bought and fewer read than any other book. You have a book there that tells you how to find God, how to live, and what lies ahead in the world to come. You are without excuse. It will be for you the sweetest book or the bitterest, depending on whether or not you heed its warnings, obey its instruction, and receive its Christ.

It is a bitter-sweet book to the Christian. When we first become Christians, God's Word is sweeter than honey and the honeycomb, but as we begin to face up to it, it makes demands of us. It separates us from the world and makes us aliens and exiles in Babylon. We shall be persecuted and misunderstood. If we try to live up to its teachings, neighbors and fellow church members will criticize because our conduct will show them up. If we preach the whole counsel of God, we shall be accused of extremism, not only by the world but also by a professing church that cannot endure sound doctrine. We shall be strangers and pilgrims on the earth, viewed with suspicion even by some "religious" people. The man who takes his Bible seriously will soon learn that there is a price to pay. He must take the bitter with the sweet.

Dr. A. J. Gordon believed and preached the second coming of Jesus Christ. His biographer says. "Advocacy of this doctrine cost him much. It seems to awaken suspicion and lead to estrangement, this great doctrine of hope. 'It is not wanted', he used to say, 'by a church with millionaire merchants and by great universities. But, after all, it was for the assertion of this doctrine that Christ at the last was crucified' (Matthew 26:64)."

When you take the Bible for your guide, you may have to renounce something you hold most dear. You may have to undertake something you do not want to do. Your whole pattern of life may be upset. You have not been called to march in a dress parade, but to endure hardness as a good soldier of Jesus Christ. The Bible is sweet to a Christian, but a diet of sweets is not good for anybody. In this day of sugar-coated Christianity, we need to learn the bitterness of repentance, persecution, and hardship. We follow a rejected Lord and we belong with him outside the gate, bearing his reproach. We cannot enjoy some things we once enjoyed. We cannot go where we used to go, or do what we used to do. We have been called to deny self, take up a cross, and follow a crucified Savior. Bible promises are sweet, but sometimes the commandments are bitter. "Having therefore these promises" we must "cleanse ourselves from all filthiness of the flesh and spirit" (2 Corinthians 7:1), and that may mean giving up evil habits, and getting right with people—restitution and reconciliation. Some receive the Word with joy but are soon offended; they cannot take the bitter with the sweet. The will of God is sometimes a bitter cup, as when our Lord told Peter by what death he should glorify God. Even our Lord prayed that his cup might pass, but for the joy set before him—the sweet—endured the cross—the bitter. Even so we must take the shadow of the cross for our abiding place as the old song says, seeking no other sunshine than the sunshine of his face. Shadow and sunshine, bitter and sweet!

All ministers need to learn early the lesson of the bittersweet book. Alexander Whyte wrote, "The true preacher may have, usually has, but few people as people go in our day and the better the preacher sometimes the smaller the flock. It was so in our Master's case. The multitude followed after the loaves but they fled from the feeding doctrines till he first tasted *that dejection and sense of defeat* which so many of his best servants are fed on in this world. Still as our Lord did not tune his pulpit to the taste of the loungers of Galilee, no more will a minister worth the name do anything else but probe deeper and deeper into the depths of truth and life as was the case with the Master till his followers, though few, will be all the more worth having."

Joseph Parker said, "The prophet whose sermon is repentance sets himself against his age and will for the time being be battered mercilessly by the age whose moral tone he challenges. There is but one word for such a man, 'Off with his head!' You had better not preach repentance until you have pledged your head to heaven."

Such a ministry will not build up crowds but it may thin them. It will not produce impressive statistics—the only yardstick most of the religious world knows anything about. As in the days of Ezekiel, people will come and hear, and will not heed, but they "... shall know that there hath been a prophet among them" (Ezekiel 2:5).

When you preach the bitter-sweet book you will get a bitter-sweet reaction. It will bring joy and gladness to all who receive it, and the looks on their faces will compensate for all the toil and effort of preparing and preaching the message. Some will resent and reject it, criticizing you, and the looks on their faces would curdle milk. You will go to your room bruised and grieved, ready like old Jeremiah to resign and run a motel in the wilderness. I warn you, if you are going to take this Bible seriously, get ready for the bitter along with the sweet. When you taste it, it will be sweet. When you swallow it, it may be bitter. Too many of us are Bible tasters; we have never swallowed it and made it our daily food. It is not glorified dessert. We will never grow robust Christians by feeding them cream puffs on Sunday morning.

The Bible is a bitter-sweet book as it relates to these days in which we live. In olden times, the watchman sat in a lonely tower, and, when asked "Watchman, what of the night?" replied, "The morning cometh and also the night" (Isaiah 21:11, 12). Now in this atomic age the watchman studies a radar screen, but the best sentinel for the ramparts we watch is the Old Book. In these frightening days it still says, "The morning cometh and also the night." It is a bittersweet prediction.

To the Christian, good news is bad news, and bad news is good news. "When they shall say, Peace and safety..." that is good news; "... sudden destruction cometh..." (1 Thessalonians 5:3): that is bad news. "Distress of nations, with perplexity;... Men's hearts failing them for fear...": that is bad news. "Look up, up lift up your heads." Don't drop your heads or shake your heads but lift up your heads, "for your redemption draweth nigh": that is good news (Luke 21:25, 28). What is bitter for the unprepared is sweet for those who are ready. When I read the fearful headlines, I do not rejoice in the misery and agony of these days; but I do rejoice for what they indicate. As bad as conditions are, they are not bad enough yet. As soon as man gets to the end of his tether, God will step in and say, "You've had it long enough, now I'll take over." "Perplexity," the state of having lost our way, is the word our Savior used. Socially, politically, economically, educationally, and even religiously, we have lost our way. Nobody in Washington can post a sign, "This Way Out," but there is his way out. The only correct interpretation of what is going on today is not coming from news commentators or historians, but from the Word of God. Whatever political significance this or that may have, what really matters is the prophetic significance.

One might as well talk nuclear physics to a monument in a city park as to discuss world events with people who know nothing of Bible eschatology. It is a waste of time; it is casting "pearls before swine" (Matthew 7:6). It is a different language and there can be no dialogue. A Ph.D. degree does not of itself qualify any man to be an expert in this field. Our Lord said, "Ye do err, not knowing the scriptures, nor the power of God" (Matthew 22:29). Without these qualifications the most brilliant scholar is in total error.

The Bible interpretation of these last days is bitter-sweet: "The morning cometh and also the night" (Isaiah 21:11, 12). Paul Harvey, discussing our moral decline, says, "It is the Christian's conviction that Christ will return and take over when mortals have made a hopeless mess of self-government. *How bittersweet this hour must be for the angels.*" Indeed, the angels must look on in wonder at the stupidity of the human race, in the graduate school scientifically and in kindergarten spiritually, trying to get to the moon when they don't know how to live on earth. As bitter as these times may be when the world is a madhouse and the inmates are trying to run the asylum, the man who knows his Bible finds it sweeter than honey. He is not of the night nor of darkness, and that day will not overtake him as a thief.

"Watch and pray" (Matthew 26:41)—and keep close to the bitter-sweet book!

The Church Within the Church

A church full of people on Sunday morning can be an inspiring sight. We can be thankful that the people are in the house of God instead of somewhere else. If they worship in spirit and in truth, it can be the greatest event of the week. We can rejoice that we live in a land where people can and do go to church. Not many would live where there are no churches, but too many Americans live as though there were no churches!

A Sunday morning congregation can be a saddening as well as a gladdening spectacle. When I have preached for a week in churches where I never see most of the Sunday morning crowd until the next Sunday, I am not thrilled on Sunday morning—I am troubled. The Lord's day crowd does not delight me; it depresses me because it indicates a Sunday morning Christianity that is the greatest hindrance to real revival. It pays God a tribute of one hour at church and then says, "Goodbye, God, I'll see you next Sunday." These Sunday morning glories, who bloom only to fold up for the rest of the week, are often a greater problem than the publicans and sinners outside the church.

It was this brand of religion that caused Isaiah to write, "Bring no more vain oblations; incense is an abomination unto me; the new moons and sabbaths, the calling of assemblies, I cannot away with; it is iniquity, even the solemn meeting" (Isaiah 1:13). It led Amos to cry, "Come to Bethel, and transgress; at Gilgal multiply transgression; and bring your sacrifices every morning, and your tithes after three years: And offer a sacrifice of thanksgiving with leaven, and proclaim and publish the free offerings: for this liketh you, O ye children of Israel, saith the Lord God" (Amos 4:5). Our Lord condemned it by quoting Isaiah "This people draw near me with their mouth, and with their lips do honor me, but have removed their heart far from me" (Isaiah 29:13). Paul had it in mind when he wrote of "a form of godliness, but denying the power thereof" (2 Timothy 3:5).

The churches of Ephesus, Sardis, and Laodicea must have had a full house on Sunday morning, but Ephesus had left its first love, Sardis had a name to be alive but was dead, and Laodicea was neither cold nor hot, but lukewarm. God was disgusted with such religiosity in Isaiah's day and our Lord was nauseated with the Laodicean congregation—rich and increased with goods and needing nothing. Is it not better to be at least warm than to be cold? Our Lord said, "No." He would have us cold or hot but never lukewarm. Better no pretense of worship at all than to play church. Our Lord called the Pharisees hypocrites and play-actors, because they substituted a performance for an experience. It is common practice on Sunday morning today. Form without force, ritual without reality; it is better to have nothing at all—better cold than lukewarm.

This much is certain: if we do not soon make church membership mean *something*, it will soon mean *nothing*. To the majority of our members, it means next to nothing already. It means less than the P.T.A., the civic club, or the fraternal order. If we do not set a new standard for church membership, we are going to be sunk by the dead weight of our unconverted and undedicated majority. The multitude of Christmas-and-Easter, Sunday-morning professing Christians could out-vote the faithful minority any time they chose to do it.

Some brave pastors are making a noble effort to do something about it. One who has had considerable success with it says it has been "a difficult and painful undertaking." It cut his membership in half. When the policy of the church is in the hands of prominent but undedicated men and women, there will naturally be an upheaval if the pastor seeks a return to the New Testament.

It is objected that we should not draw up a set of rules and regulations, since the New Testament is a sufficient rule of faith and practice. Indeed it is, but we have church covenants although few church members pay any attention to them. It is as proper to gather from the New Testament a condensed church membership platform as it is to draw up statements of faith or to prepare sermons.

Church membership means nothing to most of our members because Christian discipleship means nothing. Unless we soon put meaning into both, we shall become a lukewarm Laodicea which our Lord will spew from his mouth.

What is the answer? We can plug along with most of the membership inactive, like a lung with pneumonia and only a few of the cells breathing. That is usual procedure, and we excuse ourselves by saying things could be worse; but things could be better. Paul did not accept conditions at Corinth as normal, nor did our Lord put up with the state of affairs at Ephesus, Pergamos, Thyatira, Sardis and Laodicea. Some go to the other extreme, excommunicating delinquent members, drawing up rigid rules, and excluding all who do not come up to the standard. Others pull out with a handful of the faithful and go down the street to start a new church. Soon they have another church just like the one from which they escaped.

How did our Lord deal with Laodicea? That is a fair example and a good test case. He stood outside the door and said, "If any man (anyone) hear my voice, and open the door..." (Revelation 3:20). Dr. Campbell says Christ excommunicated the whole church and started over with one man. The way out is to begin a new church in the old church with a dedicated few who will live in fellowship with the Lord. Let this Master's minority seek to win the unfaithful majority of the old membership and beyond them, the unbelieving outside. Begin with a handful of kindling wood and the backlog will eventually burn! This will make the Wednesday night prayer meeting the real thermometer of the church instead of the Sunday morning congregation. Obsessed as we are with statistics nowadays, this is not easy to put into practice; but it is the way God works and it is the only answer.

We have been so occupied with the *extensive* that we are not disposed to emphasize the *intensive*. Not many are willing to give their time to work with small groups; however, small group movements are spreading today everywhere. Laymen's groups, prayer groups, Bible study groups—good, bad, and indifferent—are springing up in all directions. The idea is sound and scriptural, but its implementation depends on the local leadership. It is the principle of Gideon's three hundred all over again. Whether one calls it the Master's minority, or the company of the committed, or God's remnant, this is the trend.

Of course, the policy of many churches is in the hands of men and women who are not remotely interested in a spiritual New Testament church and who couldn't care less. Obviously, any effort to develop the church within the church would run into plenty of trouble. On the other hand, this church within the church must beware of becoming a self-righteous clique of super saints (and snooper-saints!), ending in a Phariseeism worse than the evil they set out to correct.

Our Lord did not say to Laodicea that if any one hear his voice and open the door, a great revival would begin. He said, "I will come in to him, and sup with him, and he with me" (Revelation 3:20). The emphasis is on fellowship of the believer with his Lord, but that *is* revival and evangelism will follow. The divine order is faith in Christ, fellowship with Christ, faithfulness to Christ, and fruitfulness for Christ. As we abide we abound, and without him we can do nothing.

Dr. A. J. Gordon said, "A few Spirit-filled disciples are sufficient to save a church. The Holy Ghost acting through these can and does bring back recovery and healing to the whole body." The church has within itself, by the Spirit, the power for reclamation and renewal; but this sort of re-creation cannot be brought about by a group of experts and high powered promotion. It is the work of God and cannot be regulated by our devices. The Savior outside Laodicea's door is not waiting for a committee to pass a resolution. He is waiting for someone to hear his voice and open a door.

The Church Within the Church

O Jesus, Thou art standing
Outside the fast-closed door,
In lowly patience waiting
To cross the threshold o'er.
Shame on us, Christian brothers,
His name and sign who bear,
O shame, thrice shame upon us,
To keep him standing there.

"A Wind From Elsewhere"

I was reading a newspaper account of an unusually bad spell of smog in Los Angeles. The city was enveloped in blinding, polluted air. The sun could not be seen at midday. Hospitals reported sharp increases in patients. Tempers were on edge as the inhabitants coughed and wheezed their way through the pall that hung over the metropolis. Politicians blamed each other; the mayor and governor exchanged sharp telegrams. It was a meteorological nightmare.

In the midst of the newspaper reports came this statement from the air pollution experts in Los Angeles: *"Only a sweep of winds from elsewhere could relieve the smog."* That set me thinking of other fogs and other winds. *The world is smog-bound.* Politically and morally, we live in a blinding haze. Conditions of low visibility prevail. Man gropes in polluted darkness. Black and white have become a smudge of indefinite gray. What was once clear is now fuzzy and indistinct. The experts are bewildered. Politicians blame each other. *Only a sweep of winds from elsewhere can relieve the smog.* Only the breath of God can dispel the miasma that grips mankind.

There are plenty of experts in Los Angeles, I am sure. Meteorologists abound, but they were all waiting for the wind to blow! It was as simple as that. The statesmen of earth are helpless in the world smog. Sociologists shake their heads. The United Nations cannot solve the riddle. Nobody in Washington knows what to do. Unlike the pollution experts in Los Angeles, they will not suggest the only remedy. Who in Washington, or London, or Moscow, or anywhere else will even hint that the answer lies in heaven? The smog has blinded them and they will not admit that they are blind leaders of the blind. All sorts of experiments are being tried: social reforms, political projects, legislation, education, reformation—none of these can lift the cloud. The winds of God must move in before the plague is conquered. The problem is sin, and neither science nor sociology has the answer to sin.

Likewise, the *church is smog-bound.* Never has the religious world been in greater confusion. Denominational leaders wring their hands. Theology is one dense fog. There are those who say that God is dead. Experts sit in symposiums and pool their ignorance. They survey the scene but have no answer. Some do not even know what the question is! Seminary students "frequent doctor and saint and hear great argument about it but evermore come out the same door wherein they went." Not many scholars will admit that only a sweep of winds from elsewhere will relieve the smog. Who is praying like Isaiah, "Oh that thou wouldest rend the heavens, that thou wouldest come down" (Isaiah 64:1)?

The country folk of my boyhood days understood better than some Ph.D.'s of today that only a divine visitation can meet our need. They sang:

> All is vain *unless the Spirit*
> Of the Holy One come down.

At Pentecost, the Spirit came with "a sound from heaven as of a mighty rushing wind" (Acts 2:2). (It is significant that the words for "wind" and "Spirit" are the same in Hebrew, Greek, and Latin.) Only a wind from elsewhere, like that, will clear our theological and spiritual smog.

There is mystery here. Our Lord said to Nicodemus, "The wind bloweth where it listeth, and thou hearest the sound thereof, but canst not tell whence it cometh, and whither it goeth" (John 3:8). This is something we cannot work up from below. We spend a lot of time in our churches these days trying to work up something that is not there! No conference of experts can produce the winds of heaven. We have all sorts of bellows to blow hot air, but all our puffing will not clear the smog; it will only add more. We must bow to the sovereignty of the Spirit who divides "severally as he will" (1 Corinthians 12:11).

This does not mean that there is anything capricious about the work of the Spirit. It does not mean that we sit with folded hands on the chance that God may or may not sometime blow upon us in revival blessing. The wind obeys certain laws, and we can discover them and abide by them. We cannot control natural winds, but we can set our sails, put up our windmills, and get in the path of the wind. We cannot produce the winds of heaven in revival blessing, but we can, for one thing, *pray* for a visitation of the Spirit upon the church. That will mean more serious praying than one hears in the average prayer meeting. It will take more than a formal day of prayer, when we mumble the same worn phrases with no indication of urgency or concern. Listen to the average church member when he is called upon to pray, and it will be evident that he has not had much practice lately.

Dr. Jonathan Goforth was to speak at a prayer meeting where attendance was pitiful. The pastor apologized and asked, "Dr. Goforth, why do people not come to pray?" The old veteran replied, "Because they don't believe God. If they really believed the Lord meets with us when we gather in his name, and if they loved him, nothing could keep them away."

Most of the things we do in church these days can be done without any special assistance from the Holy Spirit, so why bother God with praying? The tragedy today is that the situation is desperate, but the saints are not. Our Lord had much to say about desperate praying, as in the case of the importunate widow and the man with visitors at midnight and no bread. If church lights burned late at night, not at a religious hootenanny but with saints on their knees in holy desperation, God would move in answer to the prevailing prayer of his people.

Along with *prayer*, there must be *preparation*. We must get sin out of our lives, put all on the altar, and be ready like the disciples at Pentecost. There must be repentance, confession and forsaking of sin, restitution and reconciliation, making things right with people, separation from the world, and submission to the Lordship of Jesus Christ. When God's people humble themselves—and pray, and seek God's face, and turn from their wicked ways—he will hear and forgive and heal. The winds of heaven will blow when we remove obstacles, get in position, and put up our windmills.

One thing more: when revival comes, we must *participate* by *receiving* and by *sharing*. To be filled with the Spirit, we must believe and receive. Someone has said that "believe" and "receive" are two of the hardest words to spell, because it is "ie" in one and "ei" in the other. Certainly these two words are often difficult to understand in Christian experience. Yet "believe" and "receive" is the principle of the new birth (John 1:12), the law of prayer (Mark 11:24), and the basis of the Spirit-filled life (John 7:37-39). The Christian believes there is such an experience as being filled with the Spirit; he receives that filling and then believes he has received. Prayer and preparation empty the heart of sin, and then faith receives the Spirit's filling.

We must also *share*. We are not only filled; we are to overflow. From within the Spirit-filled Christian flow rivers of living water as our Lord said. I have seen too many church members "enjoy" revivals who never tried to bring anyone else to share its blessings. That is selfishness of the worst sort. If we do not overflow, we become stagnant swamps.

When the church began at Pentecost, what a smog-bound world it faced in the Roman Empire! The winds of heaven purified that world wherever they blew. The Wesleyan revival found England in a polluted fog, but the fresh breath of heaven cleared the atmosphere of that day as no social reform ever could have done. In fact, the great reforms that followed were the fruits of that revival and we still enjoy the benefits. Today we are trying to have the benefits without the revival. We are trying to air-condition this age by education and legislation, when only winds from elsewhere can clear the smog. The nation and the church are like the valley of dry bones in the book of Ezekiel, and only the winds of heaven, now as then, can make these dry bones live.

It is not enough to deplore the smog. Lectures on the wind will never stir up a breeze, but we can *pray, prepare* and *participate*. Regeneration is a miracle. We cannot produce it, but we can hear and obey God's call to repent and believe; then the Holy Spirit will perform the miracle. We cannot confess Christ as Lord or understand the Scriptures except by the Holy Spirit, but we can consent and cooperate with him. So too, revival is a supernatural visitation from above; but we can meet the conditions, and God will bless a praying and prepared people who are willing to participate.

"The Journey Is too Great"

The journey is too great for thee (1 Kings 19:7).

IT is the comforting word of the angel to rugged Elijah under the juniper. If ever a man seemed equal to any emergency, it was this granitic prophet. He was built for storm and stress. Like the New Testament Elijah, John the Baptist, he was not a reed shaken by the wind nor a wearer of soft clothing in kings' houses; but, just the same, he collapsed, and we do well to take warning.

It had been a great day on Carmel. Elijah had prayed down both fire and water and had annihilated the prophets of Baal. He was established as the champion of Jehovah in the land, but any man who calls for a showdown between Baal and the true God is in for trouble in any generation. Elijah might have advocated peaceful coexistence. Carmel would have been a great spot for a summit conference! The great prophet took a stance that exacted a terrific toll of body and mind. The next day after Carmel has put many a seer under the juniper. After our Lord's baptism came his temptation. Dr. Scroggie says, "After the dove came the devil." It was after Paul's third heaven experience that he listed his thorn in the flesh.

They had needed rain in Israel for a long time, but before the showers there must be a showdown, and before the showdown there must be a prophet. We have been singing "There Shall Be Showers Of Blessing" for years, but so far there has been only a sprinkle here and there. There will be no downpour of revival blessing until we face the issue of Baal or Jehovah. When Elijah asked, "How long halt ye between two opinions?" (1 Kings 18:21) the people answered him not a word. It is so today. Call on the average Sunday morning congregation to take a stand and there will be a profound silence.

You have all the elements of revival on Carmel. There is the prophet calling the people to God in a day of apostasy. There is the confrontation with the forces of Baal. There is the rebuilding of God's altar. After the sacrifice came supplication. Then came the fire of God's power and the flood of God's blessing. It was a great day on Carmel, but the preacher who calls his people to the test of fire had better be ready for trouble. It is easier to talk on other subjects, and a minister may save himself a trip to the wilderness and a session under the juniper.

On top of all this came the threat of Jezebel to kill the preacher. Jezebel was one of the wickedest women of all time. She had brought her heathen religion into Israel and had set up the altar of Baal beside the altar of Jehovah. Jezebel is still with us, and any prophet who calls for a showdown on Carmel will have a head-on collision with Ahab's queen. In the Book of Revelation we find a Jezebel in the church at Thyatira endeavoring to mix the church and the world—the mystery of godliness with the mystery of iniquity. Today any preacher who challenges Baal and refuses to be manipulated by Babylon infiltrating the church under the guise of recreation or social innovations will hear from Jezebel!

When Jezebel threatened Elijah, we read, "when he saw that, he arose, and went for his life" (1 Kings 19:3). The man who was accustomed to standing before the Lord God of Israel lets a wicked woman scare him almost out of his senses. We think of Simon Peter who, "when he saw the wind boisterous, was afraid" (Matthew 14:30).

This was Elijah's greatest blunder. He was on the threshold of a great revival in Israel. The prophets of Baal had been slain. The people had cried, "The Lord he is the God" (1 Kings 18:39). If Elijah had stood his ground, the seven thousand faithful believers in Israel might have rallied to him.

The history of a nation might have been changed. Many a prophet has let the devil and Jezebel scare him out of the greatest victory of his life. Sometimes pastors who dare to expose sin in the church win the first round of the battle; then the devil puts on the pressure; some prominent member gets angry, and Elijah takes off to the wilderness saying, "It is enough" (1 Kings 19:4). "I've had it," would be his words today.

God knows our frame and remembers that we are dust. The angel fed Elijah and put him to sleep. Some prophets have had too much food and sleep. God save us from overeating and oversleeping! Others have worn themselves out seeking strange experiences, when they really need food and rest. Elijah had his greatest experience of God *after* he rested. At Cherith, he learned the lesson of God's provision; at Carmel, he learned the lesson of God's power; but in the cave, he learned the lesson of God's presence as he had never known it before.

Elijah had a lot to learn. God met him at Horeb with the question, "What doest thou here, Elijah?" (1 Kings 19:9). Many a man running from his post of duty needs to hear that voice, but, instead of confessing his mistake, Elijah justifies himself, "I have been very jealous for the Lord God of hosts" (v. 1). Now every preacher ought to be jealous, not of other preachers, but for God. Paul was jealous over his Corinthian flock. God is jealous and will not share his throne with another. We ought to be jealous when we see Christians living with a divided allegiance—when Jezebel sets up an altar to Baal. A cave is a poor place for an Elijah when he should have been standing up for God against Jezebel in Samaria.

Elijah learned three lessons at Horeb. First, he learned something about *self-pity*. He lamented that the prophets had been slain ... and I, even I only, am left" (1 Kings 19:10). He was the surviving saint, with a martyr complex. Any preacher with a streak of the prophet in him is always in danger of imagining himself to be the lone survivor of a vanishing breed—the last of the old, school.

Elijah learned something about *statistics*. Good men, jealous for God, often have trouble with statistics. God had a different set of figures from Elijah's. Seven thousand in Israel had not bowed to Baal. God has a faithful remnant today. There were a few "even in Sardis," in that dead church, with an image to be alive. They may be a minority, but God knows who and where they are. Elijah should have stayed in Samaria and rallied that spearhead for God and righteousness. If God's prophets would defy Jezebel and exalt God today, his seven thousand might take heart, rise up, and be counted. There are many good people today who do not like the way things are going in state and church. We need to stand on Carmel, call for a showdown, repair God's altars, and pray down fire and water until there is the sound of abundance of rain.

Finally, Elijah learned a lesson in *stillness*. God did not speak in wind, earthquake, or fire, but in the still, small voice. Now God does speak sometimes in wind as at Pentecost, in earthquake as at the crucifixion and the resurrection, and in fire as with cloven tongues when the Spirit came; but he also speaks in a whisper. Elijah had been through days of wind, earthquake, and fire. He needed to be still and know God. It is wrong to hide in a cave in quiet solitude, cultivating our own souls, when we need to wrestle with stormy issues of our day. It is equally wrong to become so involved with controversial problems, so obsessed with the world situation, theological issues, or personal difficulties, that we have no time for communion with God.

> We are living, we are dwelling, in a grand and awful time,
> In an age on ages telling; to be living is sublime.

We can become so wrought up over movements and counter movements that we try to stay on Carmel and end in collapse.

God did not demote the wearied Elijah. After the stillness came action. He ordered Elijah to pass the torch on to his successors. What a trio he was to ordain: Hazael, Jehu, and Elisha! God has his men in the offing, and some of them are not the sort we might have chosen. Let us not try to perpetuate ourselves into the next generation. There is only one of a kind. There is only one like you, or me, for which let us be thankful! Let us serve our generation by the will of God, then anoint some Elisha to carry on where we left off. Remember that Elisha was not a second Elijah.

"The journey is too great" for all of us. If you are under the juniper, for whatever reason, press on to Horeb and get your orders; not in wind, earthquake, or fire, but in the whisper of the still, small voice.

Despising Our Youth

Let no man despise thy youth (1 Timothy 4:12).

PAUL is advising young Timothy to conduct himself in such a way that no one may look down upon him as a brash novice. Pride, overbearing zeal without knowledge, and unwise behavior can mar young preachers, especially in these days when we suffer from an epidemic of amateurism. Some of us marvel at the patience of godly souls who put up with us in our early ministry. They had reasons aplenty for despising our youth!

Recently a young minister suggested to me a secondary application of Paul's counsel to Timothy. *We can despise our own youth.* We can reach that sad state where we look down with scorn on our earlier years – when we started out, all aglow with first love, before we had met too many Bible scholars. We were on our spiritual honeymoon, and grim reality had not yet smothered our zeal. We loved the Bible and we loved the Lord, and we didn't know any better than to tell everybody about it. Like country boys come to town, we were spiritual yokels and we embarrassed sedate souls resting at ease in Zion. But we grew up and became educated, experienced, and established, and now we look with condescending distaste on the days of our youth, ashamed of our early zeal and awkward testimony.

To be sure, as we grow older, just as in married life, some of the manifestations of love change as we mature; but both in marital and spiritual experience what is often credited to maturity is really cooling of affection. If we were truthful we would have to sing:

> Where is the joy that once I knew
> When first I saw the Lord?
> Where is the soul-refreshing view
> Of Jesus and his Word?
>
> What peaceful hours I then enjoyed!
> How sweet their memory still!
> But they have left an aching void
> This world can never fill.

This business of despising one's youth reaches in all directions. Recently, a senator said that the early victories of American history were due to "reckless youth favored by an improbable run of luck." That is news to some of us who have felt that God had a hand in our young republic. If our forefathers, who signed the Declaration and fought the Revolution were just reckless and lucky, we need to rewrite our history! There is plenty of evidence that these men recognized God, however much we may try to erase him from our national life to satisfy a few atheists. The senator went on to say that America must "grow up" and "come of age." We are reminded that we started as a rural people but are now urbanized, and must get the hayseeds out of our hair, move out of the backwoods, and "get with it."

What America really needs is a rebirth of the "reckless youth" of 1776 and a new crop of true Americans. I heard General Douglas MacArthur say on his seventy-fifth birthday, "Seductive murmurs are arising that we are provincial and immature, reactionary and stupid, when we idealize our own country; that there is a higher destiny for us under another more general flag. Repudiate them in the marketplace, from the platform and pulpit!"

Sinister satanic forces are at work, nibbling away at our Constitution. The floodgates are open to communist propaganda; in the name of free speech traitors are allowed to spread their poison, seeking to take away what free speech we still have. If what I see in America is maturity, we had better get through to second childhood and recover the spirit we had before the country was overrun by lawless, demonized beatniks, crackpots, and screwballs. Our hope for survival lies in a new generation of Americans, not a motley mob of internationalists. This is no time to despise our youth!

The church can despise her youth. More than one denomination has started in a fire and ended in a fog. It is the history of Judaism, of the Reformation, and of most of our fellowships today. We are being told that we have outgrown our grass-roots beginnings and that we should forget our brush arbor camp meeting days and come of age in "progressive maturity." Now there is a healthy maturity, but what we sometimes mistake for adulthood is often comfortable middle age that precedes senility. Dr. Phillips says the church is "so prosperous that it is fat and out of breath and so organized that it is musclebound." The greatest advances of Christianity have been made in the adolescence of new movements.

The church at Ephesus despised its youth. For all its works and labor and orthodoxy, it had lost its "Amen" and its "Hallelujah," its testimony meeting and its fire. It had become a big, busy institutionalism with more wires strung and less power in them. It had "works" aplenty but not "first works"—those activities which are the spontaneous expression of love for Christ. It had left its first love, which is another way of saying it despised its youth.

Here is a peril of the young preacher, fresh out of school and starry eyed with lofty dreams of a church where Jesus Christ is taken seriously. Soon the honeymoon is over and he realizes that there is a great gulf fixed between the actual and the ideal. He may become disillusioned and leave the ministry; or he may become disgusted, read the riot act, and resign. He may accept the situation as normal; and if he cannot pull the congregation up to his standard, he may sink to theirs. If he cannot bring the regiment up to the flag, he may bring the flag back to the regiment. He despises his youth and in later years says to a flaming zealot, "Oh, yes, I used to expect miracles and pray for a New Testament church, but I got over it and you will too." I see such faces in minister's meetings. The glow is gone. They look bored when some young Timothy reminds them of the joy they have lost and the love they have left. They despise his youth because they despise their own.

Our Lord said conversion and childlikeness are the keys to the kingdom (Matthew 18:3). Christians need to be converted now and then and become children again. If not, they become childish like children playing in the marketplace. Dr. Campbell Morgan said, "Begin again as though you had never known him and with all the simplicity of a little child." We cannot turn time backward in its flight, but we can return to first love and first works. It is the first item on the agenda for most of us these days. Whatever you do, let no man, not even yourself, despise your youth!

Cleansing the Temple

THE gospel of Matthew is the gospel of the kingdom, presenting our Lord Jesus as King. In the twenty-first chapter we read about his triumphal entry into Jerusalem. It was the only time he ever took part in a public demonstration of his kingship. He had come first to the lost sheep of the house of Israel. He had come unto his own and his own received him not. On this occasion, he rode into Jerusalem on a colt, fulfilling the prophecy, "behold, thy King cometh" (Zechariah 9:9). Of course they rejected and crucified him, but on his cross hung the superscription, "Jesus of Nazareth, King of the Jews."

After the King entered Jerusalem, he cleansed the temple. There is a cleansing of the temple recorded in all four of the Gospels (Matthew 21:12-17; Mark 11:15-17; Luke 19:45, 46; John 2:13-17). He cleansed the temple at the beginning of his ministry, as John records. He found the outer court full of unholy trading in oxen, sheep, and doves. People who came to worship originally were required to bring their sacrifices, but now these offerings could be bought on the spot, and their money changed into currency required for the temple. It began innocently enough, but by the time of our Lord's visit it had become a racket, "an house of merchandise" (v. 16), as he called it. He cleaned out the place, but the reform was only temporary. When he returned at the close of his ministry, what had begun as "an house of merchandise" had become "a den of thieves" (Mark 11:7). Once again he cleared out the abominable traffic. "And the blind and the lame came to him in the temple; and he healed them" (Matthew 21:14).

This was a great moment. I wish that some artist would put it on canvas. For a brief time the temple was restored to be what it was meant to be. The King had returned and was in control. The racketeers were gone and the house of God became truly a house of prayer for all people, a place of healing and blessing. When the King is in control in his temple, that is what always takes place.

Our churches today need a new visit from the King. The church is the temple of God (1 Corinthians 3:16, 17; 1 Corinthians 6:16), built upon the foundation of the apostles and prophets, Jesus Christ himself being the chief corner stone (Ephesians 2:20-22). Peter writes, "Ye also, as lively stones, are built up a spiritual house, an holy priesthood, to offer up spiritual sacrifices, acceptable to God by Jesus Christ" (1 Peter 2:5). In this temple we offer the sacrifices of a broken spirit (Psalm 51:17), dedicated lives (Romans 12:1) and praise (Hebrews 13:15). Here, by the way, is the pattern and order of a true revival. It begins with hearts broken in repentance, lives yielded in dedication, and it produces the sacrifice of praise.

Our churches are dedicated to God. The buildings are meant to be houses of prayer for all people, where God meets with us and where men and women come to be blessed, even as the blind and the lame came to Jesus in the temple. Alas, even as in the temple of his day, so many churches are not what they were meant to be. They have become houses of merchandise; and if this condition persists, they become dens of thieves, for things tend to grow worse spontaneously if they are not turned to good designedly.

When does a church become a house of merchandise? Going in for easy religion will do it. This business of selling animals for sacrifice in the temple started innocently enough. Was it not better to buy them on the spot than to go to all the trouble of raising them? But the traffic grew until exorbitant prices were charged, and doves that sold for pennies at the outset soon sold for dollars. Easy religion is dangerous. Our forefathers used to walk to church, sit on hard benches, listen to hour-long sermons, and still they had strength enough to stand up and sing, "Work For the Night Is Coming." Now we ride to church in comfortable cars, sit in plush comfort in air-conditioned auditoriums, listen to thirty minute sermons, and then barely manage to sing "Art Thou Weary, Art Thou Languid?"

Buildings and furnishings are but a means to an end. When they become ends in themselves—when they minister only to pride and comfort—they are fast becoming houses of merchandise. When the pulpit is used to glorify the preacher, when the music only shows off the singers, when church membership only enhances community status, when the prayer house becomes a play house, and when we become more interested in recreation than in re-creation, then the church becomes a house of merchandise. When we try to run the church as though it were a business, we face this peril. Church finances are too often in the hands of men who handle God's money as a cold business proposition. Sound financial principles have their place, but unless men who carry on the affairs of the church are dedicated, Spirit-filled men, they make God's house a house of merchandise, and eventually it will be a den of thieves. Business ability alone is not enough. Just because a man is a shrewd banker or a smart treasurer in a business firm, we are not to assume that he is qualified to handle the finances of the kingdom of God. The early church appointed seven men to handle business matters, and they were "of honest report, full of the Holy Ghost and wisdom" (Acts 6:3). No man has any right to sit in a church office and handle God's money unless he is a Spirit-filled man.

The sale of animals and exchange of money in the temple started as a service, but soon the money changers began to collect commissions. When we serve God for a commission – for what we get out of it – we become merchants trafficking in holy things. There are blessings and by-products in the work of God. "It pays to serve Jesus," as the song says, but when we preach or sing or work in the church for praise, for promotion, or to exalt ourselves, and when we tithe because "it pays," then we are serving God for a commission.

If our Lord appeared in our temples today, to clear out unholy merchandise and merchants, some prominent people might be missing in some churches next Sunday. Some church offices might be empty; perhaps some pulpits vacant. Some singers would not show up in choirs, and Sunday school teachers might not appear. Some envelopes would be missing from collection plates. Many money tables would be overturned and many money changers would flee.

The only service that God accepts is the spontaneous expression of our love for Christ, whether we get paid for it or not. The early Christians collected few earthly dividends. They were out to give, not to get. Theirs was no easy religion. They were not serving God for a commission.

Whatever profanes the church and keeps it from being what God wants it to be is of this world, and should be cleared out. People came to the temple in Jerusalem to worship. They came with needy lives and hungry hearts, only to be swallowed up in all the evil commercialism of the money changers. How disillusioned they must have been! They came to the house of prayer and found a den of thieves! So today, men sometimes come to church to meet God and find only a form without force, ritual without righteousness, and unholy traffic in the things of God.

Years ago a young man attended church one Sunday morning in Pretoria, South Africa. He wrote later, "The congregation did not strike me as being particularly religious. They were not an assembly of devout souls, but appeared rather to be worldly-minded people going to church for recreation and in conformity to custom." That young man was Mahatma Gandhi. One wonders what might have happened on that Sunday morning if that church had been what it was meant to be: a house of prayer and a place of blessing.

Our churches will not be what God wants them to be until we let the King come in and cleanse his temple. Jesus Christ is the head of the church and the Lord of our lives. He is King, and there is no democracy in the kingdom of God. This is *his* church! The scribes and Pharisees objected to our Lord's presence in the temple. They considered themselves the keepers of the temple, but it was his temple. Sometimes when God wants to revive a church and cleanse it, boards and officials and prominent members object as though it were *their* church. It is *his* church! What we call revival is that blessed experience when the church lets the

King make a triumphal entry and cleanse his temple. Then, it will be no longer a house of merchandise and a den of thieves, but a house of prayer and a place of blessing; and the blind and lame will come and be healed.

Observe further, that on this blessed occasion the little children shouted "Hosanna to the Son of David" (Matthew 21:15). When the King cleanses his temple there will be joy as childlike Christians sing his praises. The kingdom is for the converted and the childlike (Matthew 18:3), and revival sets them rejoicing. You will observe that there was excitement and there was emotion on this occasion. We low-rate "feeling" in our Christianity and make much of the fact that the word is not found in the New Testament in connection with Christian experience; but you will find plenty about joy and gladness. Only the priests and scribes were unhappy when our Lord was in the temple. They resented the rejoicing of the children, and our Lord asked them, "have ye never read, Out of the mouths of babes and sucklings thou hast perfected praise?" (Matthew 21:16). We read that when they saw the wonderful things that he did and the children rejoicing, "they were sore displeased" (v. 15). It is hard to believe that religious people could be so calloused to real happiness, but I have seen something like that in church revivals. There never was a spiritual awakening that did not set Christians singing—and Pharisees grumbling! During the Welsh Revival, some church people feared a wave of insanity! Some modern priests and scribes might well get excited over the insanity we already have!

How does the King cleanse his temple today? Here is where you and I come in. The church is made of people, and the church is cleansed when we are cleansed. Too many church members, it has been said, have been starched and ironed before they have been washed! Our bodies are the temples of the Holy Spirit. We need to remember in this present-day wave of church building that God dwells not in temples made with hands. Unless we bring to church the temples of our bodies, sanctified and meet for the Master's use, God will not meet with us even though we gather in a church as big as the Pentagon.

Our King wants his church to be a purified church. When he was on earth, he was consumed with the zeal of God's house. Even as a lad in the temple he had said, "Did you not know that I must be in my Father's house?" (Luke 2:49 RSV). He "loved the church and gave himself for it; That he might sanctify and cleanse it with the washing of water by the word, That he might present it to himself a glorious church, not having spot, or wrinkle, or any such thing; but that it should be holy and without blemish" (Ephesians 5:25-27).

He wants the temples of our bodies to be dedicated to him. It is our sacrifice (Romans 12:1). In the days of the Jerusalem temple, if an offering did not pass inspection by the high priest, it was not accepted. Does your offering meet the approval of the Great High Priest, our Lord himself? Is there anything in body, mind, or spirit that grieves the Holy Spirit?

> The shelf behind the door,
> The shelf behind the door;
> Tear it down and throw it out,
> Don't use it anymore;
> For Jesus wants his temple clean
> From ceiling to the floor;
> He even wants that little shelf
> That's hid behind the door.

I have read of a dilapidated little shop whose owner was about to go out of business. The floor was unswept, the windows unwashed, the goods in disorder, and the proprietor careless and untidy. One day the king came by and saw the wretched condition of the establishment. He said to the shopkeeper, "If you will do as I say, I will let you put over the door, 'Approved By The King.'" The proprietor gladly consented. Everything was changed: the floors were swept, the windows washed, the goods put in order, and the keeper himself cleaned up. Soon customers began to come and money rang in the till, because over the door was written the approval of the king.

Have you ever let the King take over that you might be a workman approved unto God? Has your prayer ever been,

> Lord Jesus, I long to be perfectly whole;
> I want Thee forever to live in my soul.
> Break down every idol, cast out every foe;
> Now wash me and I shall be whiter than snow.

Let the King cleanse and control his temple that you may offer the threefold sacrifice of a broken heart, a yielded life, and the fruit of your lips giving thanks to his Name!

Bringing Back the King

Why speak ye not a word of bringing the king back? (2 Samuel 19:10).

THE text is from the last sad years of King David. Absalom, his handsome and well beloved son, has rebelled against his father to suffer violent death at the hands of Joab. King David has been forced to leave his throne and flee for safety. It was not his first experience as a fugitive, but it was his saddest. Absalom, however, was slain, and now it is time for the King to return. It is the subject of conversation throughout all Israel.

David is particularly concerned that he be invited to return by his own tribe of Judah. He wants to come back by invitation in kingly fashion, and he has to send word to the priests to speak to the elders saying, "Why are ye the last to bring the king back to his house?" (v. 11). He has to remind them further, "Ye are my brethren, ye are my bones and my flesh: wherefore then are ye the last to bring back the king?" (v. 12).

It must have been embarrassing to David. His own people of Judah, and especially the priests and elders, should have taken the initiative and should have been the first immediately to invite the king back to his throne. They had to be reminded and prodded by the king himself to do their very obvious duty.

Leaving the story now, we proceed to apply this text to David's greater Son, our Lord Jesus Christ. He too was of the tribe of Judah. He came to his own people and his own received him not, but he is to return one day to reign not only on David's throne, but as King of kings and Lord of lords. At present he is away; but before he went away, he promised to return. During his absence, there have been many would-be usurpers. We have been plagued with plenty of Absaloms. We have joined with this upstart and that, and the pages of history are filled with the scheming, rebellion, and delusion of pretenders to the throne. Men have been weaned away from the true King by one Absalom after another, and they will continue to be until the very last usurper, Antichrist himself, shall claim to be king of kings.

Of one thing we are certain, however: every one of these counterfeits is doomed to defeat and destruction. The higher they climb the harder they fall, and there never will be peace and safety on this wretched earth until he shall return whose right it is to reign. Return he will, and that blessed event could happen at any time.

Just here emerges one of the saddest questions in our modern world. If the King of Glory is to return to reign forever, one would think such wondrous news would be on every tongue. One would expect the street corners to buzz with such a topic of conversation. It would seem that telephones would hum with such a theme, and that all our gatherings would find men and women discussing such a momentous event. Alas, one feels like walking the streets and asking chattering groups, all excited over trifles and facts, "Why speak ye not a word of bringing back the King?"

What is the explanation of this phenomenon? When Jesus came to earth the first time, there were three great world forces: the Roman world of government, the Greek world of culture, and the Hebrew world of religion; yet none of these was looking for the King. The mighty Roman world of government had accomplished wonders. It had welded the world together to some degree, linked much of it with highways, and maintained some semblance of law and order; but government had failed to meet the problem of sin and humanity wallowed in iniquity.

The Greek world had created a culture of which it has been said, "Two centuries of ancient Athens produced men who, in statesmanship, philosophy, letters, oratory, and art, set standards for all subsequent time." Yet the world was reeking in filth and corruption when Jesus came.

The Hebrew world had given to man the worship of one God, the Mosaic law, and the highest standards of righteousness. Yet the world knew not God and worshiped gods of its own.

Into such a world the King came, only to be rejected by even his very own; yet as he died on Calvary, his superscription, written in the three languages of these three worlds—Roman, Greek and Hebrew—proclaimed, him a King.

Today we have the world of government, the world of culture, and the world of religion. It is time for the King to return, but you will listen in vain to hear any of these worlds speak a word of bringing back the King. Do you catch the faintest whisper of it from the world of government? Statesmen and diplomats huddle the world around to plot and plan the world of tomorrow, but the only one who can unscramble this mess and assemble this worldwide jigsaw puzzle is left outside the door. In the United States Senate, or the conferences of the United Nations, or the get-togethers of the Big Four at Versailles, or the Big Three at Yalta, or the Big Two at Vienna—why speak they not a word of bringing back the King? Certainly the world of government has failed to solve our problems. We merely exchange one dilemma for another on our way to the World State of the Antichrist, the worst of all. We get rid of this dictator and that, but we are on our way to the worst tyrant of all time. Man is not capable of governing himself and will not submit to the government of the Son of God.

Listen to the modern world of culture, and you will never hear a word of bringing back the King. Are they looking for him in our universities? Is modern education getting ready to welcome him? If you should rise in any academic convocation and propose the return of Christ as the solution of the world's headache and heartache, you would be viewed as a crackpot; yet you need only to read the literature, look at the art, and study the culture of this age to know that man, by his wisdom, has not only failed to know God, but he has descended to a moral and spiritual state beneath the dignity of the beasts of the field. The world of culture flounders in a cesspool of iniquity.

Is the modern world of religion looking for the King? Millions in heathendom bow before sticks and stones. Other millions have their great religious systems with no place for Jesus.

The world of religion has not solved the need of the soul of man, for there are more lost souls today than in all history, and the heathen multiply faster than ever.

You will remember that King David was concerned that his own tribe of Judah should welcome him home. Today one feels like turning to the Jews, to that nation "of whom as concerning the flesh Christ came" (Romans 9:5), to ask them, "Why speak ye not a word of bringing back *your* king?" There was a day when their King was on trial and their chief priests cried, "We have no king but Caesar" (John 19:15). From that day to this, they have known one Absalom after another. They have suffered as no other race on God's earth; but when Jesus hung on the cross, his superscription read, "Jesus of Nazareth the King of the Jews," for so he is. This poor plagued people shall yet look on him whom they have pierced and receive him as their sovereign. Some of them as individuals so look for him now; but there must come a day when all Israel shall be saved, for David's Son must reign in Jerusalem.

I press on to the saddest of all applications of our text. If the world has refused the King up to now, certainly one would expect to find plenty of conversation in the church about bringing back the King. It surely was a lively subject among the early Christians. Alas, one can sit in many a mighty religious assembly, day after day, and never know that the King is coming back again. One may listen to hours and hours of addresses and discussions about the fix we're in, hearing religious panaceas proposed ad infinitum, and never will a word be spoken of bringing back the King. Here is the saddest spectacle in the church today, and one feels like standing in many a gathering of the King's own people to ask, "Why speak ye not a word of bringing back the King?"

Of course one hears much about bringing in the kingdom, but nothing of bringing back the King. Kingdom work, kingdom causes, kingdom ideals—all this we hear; but let one speak of the King's return and he is viewed out of the corner of the eye suspiciously, as though he had brought up a very troublesome subject. Some dear brother is sure to remark that it is a controversial subject. Well, any doctrine of the Christian faith is controversial. Other Bible themes have not been ignored because they are controversial.

To be sure, as with any other doctrine, some have gone overboard on the matter and have majored on prophecy, until they need to be balanced as did the Thessalonians of old. I am also persuaded that with most Christians today the devil has never had more success with any of his designs than with this, and that he has silenced the lips of believers on bringing back the King. It is almost inconceivable that any truth as clear and as frequent from the lips of our Lord should be on so few Christian lips today. It is amazing that the blessed hope which shows up on almost every page of the New Testament, and which was so great a part of early Christian faith, should be ignored as though it were a questionable quirk. In our church gatherings we easily get hot and bothered and talk aplenty about matters of far less importance. We are past masters at bewailing the times, discussing the status quo, and debating ways and means. The devil is happy to have it so, if it will keep us from speaking a word of bringing back the King.

Someone may ask, "But what good would it do to talk about the King's return? That is God's business, and he will take care of it in his own time and way. All that we can do is to be ready." That is a very popular argument today, but the New Testament Christians were not content merely to be ready. They loved the King's return; they looked for it, and they lived in the light of it.

There is no use denying it: one fails to find in much of our religious world today the *love of his appearing*. What we love usually manages to get into our conversation. What is down in the well of the heart will come up in the bucket of the speech. When men refuse to speak of bringing back the King, either they do not love it or they are not prepared for it. There is indeed an academic speculation about the doctrine that can be almost as cold as the denial of the doctrine; but usually when men love to speak of bringing back the King, they love his appearing.

The early Christians *looked* for his return. Preparation was accompanied by expectation. It is true that Jesus did not return during their lifetime, but no one is mistaken when he lives as though he might come anytime. It is always proper to live, looking for that blessed hope, and remembering that unto them that look for him, he shall appear the second time without sin unto salvation.

These believers *lived* in the light of the Lord's return. What good does it do to speak much of his appearing? Well, for one thing, "every man that hath this hope in him purifieth himself, even as he is pure" (1 John 3:3), and we are sadly in need of cleansing ourselves from all filthiness of the flesh and spirit, perfecting holiness in the fear of God. That is what revival means, and surely we need revival.

Also, when men love his appearing and look for him, they make good witnesses, missionaries, and evangelists. All one needs to do to prove that is to check the list of God's servants who have been most greatly used as ambassadors of Christ and fishers of men.

It is indeed a strange and sinister silence that has fallen over so much of the church today, that so many who name the name of Christ speak not a word of his return. We can understand why the world is dumb because it is also blind—blinded by the gods of this age to all the revelation of God; but remember that David's greatest worry, in the passage with which we started, was that his own kinsmen of Judah should be the last to welcome him. Have you noticed the words he used? "Ye are my brethren, my bones and my flesh" (2 Samuel 19:10). Does not that remind you of another verse, "For we are members of his body, of his flesh, and of his bones" (Ephesians 5:30). If it grieved David that his kinsmen in the flesh should be so slow to speak of his return, what must our Lord think of us, the members of his body the church, when we speak not a word to welcome him again? May God loosen the strings of our tongues and make us all members of his reception committee!

Bringing Back the King

Why say ye not a word of bringing back the King?
Why speak ye not of Jesus and his reign?
Why tell ye of his kingdom and of its glorious reign
But nothing of his coming back again?
Dost thou not want to look upon his loving face?
Dost thou not want to see him glorified?
Wouldst thou not hear his welcome and in that very place
Where years ago we saw him crucified?
O hark! Creations' groans, how can they be assuaged?
How can our bodies know redemptive joy?
How can the war be ended in which we are engaged
Until he come the lawless to destroy?
"Why speak ye not a word of bringing back the King?"

To obtain additional copies of this book, and to see a list of
other great Christian titles, visit our web site:
www.KingsleyPress.com

Made in the USA
San Bernardino, CA
15 January 2018